FIREFIGHTING

FIREFIGHTING

Heroes of fire and rescue through history and around the world

NEIL WALLINGTON

southwater

This edition is published by Southwater

Southwater is an imprint of
Anness Publishing Ltd
Hermes House, 88–89 Blackfriars Road
London SE1 8HA

tel. 020 7401 2077; fax 020 7633 9499

www.southwaterbooks.com; info@anness.com

© Anness Publishing Ltd 2005

UK agent: The Manning Partnership Ltd
6 The Old Dairy, Melcombe Road
Bath, BA2 3LR
tel. 01225 478444; fax 01225 478440
sales@manning-partnership.co.uk

UK distributor: Grantham Book Services Ltd
Isaac Newton Way, Alma Park Industrial Estate
Grantham, Lincs NG31 9SD
tel. 01476 541080: fax 01476 541061
orders@gbs.tbs-ltd.co.uk

North American agent/distributor:
National Book Network, 4501 Forbes Boulevard
Suite 200, Lanham, MD 20706
tel. 301 459 3366; fax 301 429 5746
www.nbnbooks.com

Australian agent/distributor:
Pan Macmillan Australia
Level 18, St Martins Tower
31 Market St, Sydney, NSW 2000
tel. 1300 135 113; fax 1300 135 103
customer.service@macmillan.com.au

New Zealand agent/distributor:
David Bateman Ltd, 30 Tarndale Grove
Off Bush Road, Albany, Auckland
tel. (09) 415 7664; fax (09) 415 8892

A CIP catalogue record for this book is available
from the British Library.

Publisher: Joanna Lorenz
Editorial Director: Helen Sudell
Project Editor: Simona Hill
Designer: Mike Morey
Editorial Reader: Jeremy Nichols
Production Controller: Darren Price

Previously published as part of a larger volume,
*The World Encyclopedia of Fire Engines
and Firefighting*

10 9 8 7 6 5 4 3 2 1

Acknowledgements

The author wishes to thank the following for their assistance and technical advice
during the preparation of this book: Ron Bentley, Eric Billingham, Gary Chapman,
Maurice Cole, Detlef Gerth, Mike Hebbard, Andrew Henry, Jerry Hepworth,
Chris Jackson, Simon Rowley, S W Stevens-Stratten, Keith Wardell. Thanks to the
Chief Officers and uniformed personnel, including photographers of many fire
bridgades including: British Airports Authority, Cheshire, Cleveland (UK), Cornwall,
Devon, Dorset, Essex, Greater Manchester, Hampshire, Humberside, Kent,
Lancashire, Leicestershire, Lincolnshire, London, Mid and West Wales, New Orleans
(Captain Chis Mickel), Wiltshire, West Midlands Fire Service (Edward Ockenden)
and West Yorkshire Fire Service (Brian Saville and Andrew Henson). Eurotunnel,
The UK Fire Protection Association, and a number of fire engine manufacturers listed
in the book. The librarians of the London Fire Brigade Library and the Fire Service
College Library, England. Simona Hill of Anness Publishing for all her hard work and
editorial guidance. And lastly my wife Susie, who has given unstinting amounts of
practical help and encouragement throughout the marathon compilation of this book.

The publishers would like to thank the following for their generous assistance:
Shane Mackichan, Andrew Henry, Shaun Ryan, Steven Schueler and Jerry Sires.

Note

In describing various fire engines throughout this book, a fire engine may be
described, for example, as a 1990 Dennis F127/Saxon/Simon ST240 24m/78ft aerial
platform ladder. The first reference (a Dennis F127) refers to the make of the fire
engine's chassis/cab; the second to the bodybuilding company; and the third
reference is to the manufacturer of the aerial ladder assembly and mechanism fitted.

CONTENTS

INTRODUCTION

One of man's oldest friends, and most deadly enemies, is fire. Ever since humans first learned to kindle a flame, fire, in an uncontrolled form, has always posed a dangerous threat to life and property. Early communities learned to respect the awesome power of fire and feared the consequences of its ferocity when it was out of control.

The beginning of socially organized firefighting can be traced back to the second century BC when a primitive attempt was made to produce a hand pump that was able to hold a quantity of water, and then direct and pump it in a modest jet on to an outbreak of fire. Little could be done to extinguish a large fire that was burning out of control, except to leave it to finish its course, or be extinguished by rain.

The first comprehensive fire brigade came into being during the Roman Empire when a dedicated corps of firefighters was formed. But it was probably not until after the devastation of the Great Fire of London in 1666 that significant developments came about in world firefighting techniques, together with more effective hand-pumped fire engines. In the mid-seventeenth century, the first British insurance companies began to form their own fire brigades. These were based in the burgeoning cities, and often more than one existed in the same locality. The flaw of this organization was

■ BELOW LEFT *This c.1900 American Amoskeag horse-drawn, steam-driven pump makes an impressive sight as it thunders towards a fire call.*

■ BELOW *New Orleans fire crews put their powerful water jets to work during a major fire.*

■ BOTTOM *A nineteenth-century London street scene as firemen set their steam pump to work amid crowds of excited onlookers.*

■ ABOVE *This 1987 Seagrave 32m/105ft articulated aerial ladder is a good example of twentieth-century American fire engine development and technology.*

that the firefighters were only obliged to help fight fire at properties insured by their own organization, leading to a farcical situation of firefighters attending a fire, only to turn away, leaving the flames burning because the property was insured by a different company.

America, too, was awakening to the risk of fire, and by the 1730s several new cities had formed volunteer fire brigades. Napoleon Bonaparte also assigned a whole division of the French army to the additional role of firefighting, and by 1800 Paris could boast 30

■ RIGHT *A modern 4x4 airport foam tender equipped with a roof-top telescopic Snozzle boom, which is capable of penetrating the fuselage of a burning aircraft, and projecting a cooling water/foam spray inside.*

powerful horse-drawn manual pumps. In 1824 Edinburgh, Scotland, became the first city to create a properly trained and equipped municipal fire brigade.

The arrival in 1829 of the world's first steam-powered fire pump built by two London-based inventors led to far more sophisticated and effective firefighting practices. By 1860, steam fire pumps were in widespread use in Great Britain and America, as well as in Russia, Denmark, India, Spain, and New Zealand. However, major fires still occurred and caused large-scale death and destruction. In 1871 a fire in Chicago, USA, soon took fearsome hold of part of the city and burned for 24 hours before coming under control. More than 300 people lost their lives and 100,000 more were made homeless. The fire-damaged area stretched for over 10 sq km/4 sq miles.

It was the coming of the motor age in the early twentieth century that ultimately revolutionized firefighting and led to the development of efficient fire brigades throughout the world. Although the first fire pump to be powered by a petrol engine had been built in Austria in 1888, the first truly self-propelled motorized fire engine was built for a north London brigade in 1904, and from then on, fire engine manufacturers grew rapidly across Europe and the United States.

As the populations of the world's cities and towns grew, the risk of fire in the many grossly overcrowded urban tenements and dwellings increased, and the incidence of fire continued to be a regular threat to life and property. Firefighting vehicles and equipment were continually being developed to meet the new challenges faced by fire brigades. Taller aerial ladders for high-rise firefighting and rescue evolved, and the first breathing apparatus sets were introduced to allow fire crews to work amid the thickest toxic smoke. Breathing sets also allowed firefighting tactics to become more aggressive as firefighters were able to

■ BELOW LEFT *This executive jet overshot the runway at Eastleigh Airport, UK, during a thunderstorm in May 1993 and landed straddling the M27 motorway. Fortunately, there were no serious injuries.*

■ BELOW RIGHT *Firefighting in the winter months can test a firefighter's endurance to the limit. This Canadian crew are encrusted with ice as they tackle a fire at St. Augustin in Quebec.*

■ ABOVE *Firefighters feel the heat as they get to work at a fire at a large disused woollen mill.*

enter burning, smoke-filled buildings, rather than stand outside projecting jets of water on to the fire to restrict its spread.

In addition, the growth and development of the industrial world brought new risks. Until the beginning of the twentieth century, almost all fires were tackled with water, but as petrochemical and other manufacturing industries increased, and different fire hazards were introduced, the use of foam and other special extinguishants, such as dry powders, were developed to deal with fires involving flammable fuels and hazardous materials.

The rapid development in worldwide mass transport systems has led to an increasing frequency of non-fire crashes, accidents and emergencies. As a result, fire brigades have had to be equipped and trained to deal with challenging and often protracted rescue incidents. It is a fact that most brigades now physically rescue more imperilled people from non-fire emergencies such as road and rail crashes, machinery accidents and weather-related emergencies, than they do from fires.

Since the terrorist attacks in the United States of America on 11 September 2001, modern-day fire crews are constantly on standby to respond to the terrorist threat. Preparations for any chemical attack involves the use of protective clothing, and fire crews are trained to decontaminate a large number of members of the public.

Nowadays even though fire brigades spend time and resources educating the public about fire safety and prevention, the human and fiscal cost of fire continues to escalate in every continent across the world. All this means that the contemporary firefighter has to be master of a wide range of skills, as well as an understanding of fire combustion and behaviour, building construction, physics and chemistry, hydraulics, psychology, and often medical issues. Modern fire and rescue work is a dangerous business and calls for a high degree of physical strength, fitness and courage. After all, when firefighters are called to the scene of an emergency, the public are usually fleeing in the other direction.

The challenges facing the world's firefighters, be they professional or volunteer, operating in densely populated city centres, or rural locations, have never been greater. To respond effectively, fire crews must train constantly under realistic conditions to be ready at any time, and in all weather conditions, to respond to requests for assistance.

Fire, accident and other emergencies are rarely out of the news headlines. Around the globe, the men and women of the world's fire and rescue services stand ready to face any dire emergency situation.

FIREFIGHTING THROUGH HISTORY

Fire engines are among the most glamorous and high-profile vehicles on the public highway. Bright conspicuous colours, strobe warning lights and various warning wailers and hooters make these firefighting machines truly awesome pieces of equipment. The highly trained crews that operate these machines inhabit an exciting and often dangerous world, as they tackle a range of emergencies and disasters both minor and major. This section explores the history and development of the fire service and firefighting skills, from the first makeshift attempts at organized firefighting to the high-tech systems and specialized machines and equipment of today.

■ OPPOSITE *A 29m/95ft Baker Aerialscope tower ladder on a Mack chassis of Brockton, Massachusetts, gets to work at a big mill fire in New England.*

■ LEFT *Bush fires present firefighters with diverse and enormous challenges. Here, two American pumpers face a wall of flames during a serious outbreak.*

The story of firefighting

As soon as human beings discovered fire it became necessary to find ways of fighting the devastating flames whenever they got out of control. The first organized attempts at firefighting began at the time of the Roman Empire, albeit in a primitive way, but it was not until the seventeenth century, despite some devastating fires, that firefighting methods really started to develop. Manually pumped fire engines, pulled at first by hand, then drawn by horses, were soon followed by steam power and the emergence of properly organized fire brigades. The arrival of the internal-combustion engine heralded huge strides in both engine evolution and firefighting methods. Today, firefighting keeps abreast of a rapidly changing world and new technology, and the service has evolved into the world's major rescue organization.

THE NATURE OF FIRE

Through the ages human beings have regarded fire with a combination of awe and terror. It has always been an essential part of human existence, and for millennia people relied on it for warmth, for cooking their food and for keeping wild and predatory animals at bay, at least while the flames burned bright during the darkest hours. The flames also provided light and a relatively comfortable area around which families and other groups could gather. Fire was also important in the development of the use of metals, for it had the power to transform them into all manner of useful tools and equipment. Conversely, fire could also be used as a weapon of war to strike panic and destruction in an opponent's camp.

With all its inherent power, it is hardly surprising that from the earliest times, the almost magical properties of fire gave rise to many myths and much folklore. The Greek god of fire, especially of the blacksmith's fire, was

Hephaestus, and his symbol was a fan of flickering flames. In due course, the Romans adopted Hephaestus as one of their own gods, attaching to him the myth and cult of fire under the title of Vulcan.

■ ABOVE *Vulcan, the Roman god of fire and blacksmiths, held the secret of working metal.*

■ BELOW *In the past, fire has been used as a weapon of war.*

■ BELOW *The awesome power of fire figures prominently in this dramatic impression of Hell by Hieronymus Bosch (1450–1516).*

■ ABOVE *To continue burning fire relies on fuel, heat and oxygen being present.*

■ RIGHT *Ceremonial fire walkers overcome the pain of burning embers in this early engraving.*

■ BELOW *Constable recorded the magnitude of this major fire in nineteenth-century London, viewed from Hampstead Heath.*

The way that fire behaves and spreads is what makes it so dangerous. From a purely scientific standpoint, for a fire to occur three separate factors must be present: fuel, which is something that will burn, a high-temperature source of ignition, and oxygen. Once a fire has been started, it can spread easily and quickly in a number of ways. Direct burning is when flames spread to combustible material directly alongside and in contact with what is already

on fire. Heat generated from a fire can travel laterally through the air (radiation) and be sufficient to ignite material remote from the original outbreak. When heat travels along solid materials (conduction), such as metal beams and joists, it can ignite combustible materials well away from the initial fire. Finally, heat and products travelling upwards from a fire (convection) can set alight anything combustible above the original outbreak.

Ever since people first learned to live with fire, it has been a potential threat to human life and property, for once flames take hold they can easily kill and wreak devastation. The fumes that fire creates can kill just as easily as the flames. Even small fires in their very early stages can produce large volumes of smoke, particularly when modern man-made materials are burning. In most fire situations, this smoke will be the killer, almost certainly quickly asphyxiating its victims long before the flames reach them. It also has a damaging material effect on personal possessions, the fabric of a home or workplace, and can be a potential threat to livelihood. Smoke levels can increase rapidly by the minute as a fire develops unchecked, as will temperatures and the rapid spread of the fire inside a building. In order for firefighters to successfully carry out rescues and tackle a spreading blaze, therefore, it is imperative that they get to the scene as quickly as possible.

■ **ABOVE LEFT** *Heat has travelled across the road by radiation to ignite the grass verge.*

■ **ABOVE CENTRE** *Metal-frame buildings aid the spread of fire.*

■ **ABOVE RIGHT** *Convection carries curling flames upwards to ignite combustible materials above the original fire.*

■ **BELOW LEFT** *Water thrown on a fat fire scatters the flames.*

■ **BELOW RIGHT** *A chip pan that has caught fire is the cause of many a kitchen conflagration.*

ACCIDENTAL OR MAN-MADE FIRE

In the past most fires were due to carelessness. It is easy to imagine how sparks from a fire in a prehistoric camp might have floated up in the hot convection current to drop down and ignite a nearby patch of dry grass. Suddenly, flames spread rapidly and a bush or forest fire erupted, threatening everything in the area and causing panic. Today many devastating bush and forest fires are caused in the same way – by a poorly tended bonfire or a thoughtlessly discarded match or cigarette.

Fire has always been a major threat to dwellings constructed of timber and thatch. In medieval Europe, such dwellings were built in close proximity, so a fire in one soon moved along an entire street. Not only were candles

and waxed torches widely used to provide lighting, but it was then common practice to light fires indoors for cooking and heating. Even though some primitive chimney flues were provided, fires frequently broke out on the underside of roofs, often spreading with frightening speed to neighbouring roofs.

The Great Fire of London in 1666 is just one of many that have swept through bustling commercial cities. It started in a baker's shop in Pudding Lane and after just five hours had spread to engulf more than 300 houses and businesses. The flames raged in three directions, running from one building to its neighbour and leaping across the narrow streets. A total lack of any fire precautions meant that nothing whatsoever stood in the way of the flames, which continued to rage for four days and destroyed four-fifths of the old City of London. After the Great Fire, timber was banned as a construction material in London in favour of brick.

By the nineteenth century, many serious and often fatal fires repeatedly caused devastation in the growing urban areas around the developing world, where poor social housing conditions were widespread. Long after the arrival of electricity there was still much use of candles, gas lighting, open-hearth fires for cooking, and oil stoves for heating. Chimneys, too, often went unswept. All these conditions helped fuel rapid spread once an outbreak of fire occurred.

In spite of improved fire safety awareness and regulations, we are still vulnerable to accidental fire. High on the list of causes are faulty or misused electrical equipment, the careless disposal of cigarettes, a general lack of care and attention while using cooking stoves and equipment, and unsupervised

■ ABOVE *The fire that spread rapidly through this disused woollen mill forced the firefighting crews working inside the building to withdraw for their own safety.*

■ BELOW *Rural fires such as this grassland and forest fire can be protracted affairs when water supplies are scarce and the affected area is extensive.*

children playing with matches. Another cause of fire, and one that is on the increase, is arson.

Compared to man-made fires, natural ones are relatively rare, but when they do occur they can be devastating. Spontaneous combustion triggered by prolonged intensely hot periods can lead to forest and bush fires that burn for weeks on end, destroying vast areas of natural habitat and sometimes engulfing towns and villages. The periodic eruption of volcanoes and the resultant red-hot lava flows can also ignite large tracts of adjacent vegetation.

THE FIRST FIREFIGHTERS

The earliest historical reference to firefighting indicates that first efforts are likely to have taken place in the second century BC, when an Alexandrian named Ctesibus invented a primitive hand-operated squirt that could throw a modest jet of water on to a fire. Resembling a large syringe, it was simply a narrow-bore parallel cylinder, about 1m/3ft in length, with a nozzle at one end and an internal piston connected to a handle at the other end. When in use, the nozzle was immersed in a bucket of water and the handle was slowly drawn out to its maximum travel. This sucked a charge of water into the squirt that was then discharged as a water jet on to the fire by pushing the handle back into the cylinder. However, such squirts would have had little impact on an outbreak of fire, and it can be assumed that in pre-Roman times fires were extinguished only when the burning material was completely consumed, a natural firebreak occurred, or when heavy rain fell.

In the early days of the Roman Empire, there are recorded examples of fire tragedies and destruction on a huge scale. For instance, during AD6 a single conflagration destroyed a quarter of all the buildings in central Rome, and it is probable that the origins of organized

firefighting can be traced back to the aftermath of this particularly destructive outbreak. The steady growth of the Roman Empire saw increasing numbers of people living collectively in cities and towns, so it would have been in everyone's interest to minimize such devastating occurrences.

Emperor Augustus recognized immediately that more effective firefighting measures were needed, and undertook to provide the population of ancient Rome with a greater level of protection from the ravages of fire. He formed a dedicated firefighting corps of men,

■ LEFT *A contemporary print shows a typical early seventeenth-century fire squirt in action. To produce a firefighting water jet, the squirt had to be held by two men while being operated by a third. It would have been filled from the buckets lying in the foreground.*

■ BELOW LEFT *Chinese firemen work primitive manual pumps supplied by bucket chains as they fight a fire in old Peking. A team of firemen with pole-mounted hooks are standing by ready to pull burning material from the buildings.*

■ BELOW RIGHT *As this medieval manuscript illustrates, fire was used early on as a maritime weapon of war.*

known as *vigiles*, who underwent training before being formed into companies based at the fire stations that soon ringed the city. *Vigiles* wore a uniform of a toga and sandals and were under the command of a *siphonarias* (officer). Their duties were primarily to provide fire patrols throughout Rome, especially at night, and to deal immediately with small fires using bucket chains – lines of vigiles and helpers who passed buckets of water from person to person from a water source to the fire and back again. This system was a much more efficient way of delivering water to a fire than if each person walked or ran all the way carrying a bucket. Some companies of vigiles were given the job of pulling down burning buildings that stood in the path of a fire to create a firebreak, or to secure access into roof areas of buildings for other vigiles to direct their bucket chains and water squirts.

Vigiles also carried an assortment of other equipment, including ladders, axes, fire blankets, hammers, various iron tools, and primitive scaffolding to enable them to reach the upper levels of buildings. They were even supplied with sponges to clean up after a fire had been extinguished. Companies of *vigiles* subsequently appeared in many parts of the Roman Empire, where active fire prevention was constantly practised.

■ ABOVE LEFT
Contemporary firefighters demonstrate a bucket chain in operation.

■ ABOVE RIGHT *As seen in this fifteenth-century print, late medieval firefighting methods were still basic.*

■ BELOW *The Fire of Rome, July AD64, painted by Hubert Robert (1733–1808), raged for three days.*

Despite all this effort Rome and other parts of the empire were subjected to some huge fires. A major outbreak in Rome in AD64 blazed for three days and nights, while in AD120 a fire swept through much of Londinium's (Roman London) structure. In truth, once a serious fire took hold, there was little anyone could do to stop it.

With the demise of the Roman Empire, it seems incredible that the basic fire-protection advances made during that period were lost, for after this time history does not record much

organized firefighting effort. The emphasis at this time was on salvage work and the recovery of personal possessions, letting fires go uncontrolled until they burned themselves out and died down after consuming everything in their path. In Britain, great fires destroyed large parts of Canterbury in AD619 and AD624. London experienced further huge conflagrations in AD798 and AD982.

HISTORICAL ACTION

In 1086, some basic attempts were made in Britain to create a general awareness of fire and its dangers. A nightly curfew was ordered requiring the covering of open fires and candles, but this rule proved unpopular and was often disregarded. In 1189 the first Lord Mayor of London, Henry Fitzalwin, issued a local law requiring new buildings to be better spaced and constructed of stone with slate or clay roofs rather than the usual combustible wood-and-straw structures of the time. However, none of these measures prevented fires from breaking out. The first Great Fire of London, in 1212, spread across the Thames and is estimated to have claimed a staggering 3,000 lives. Fire was a common hazard in other English cities of the time; Peterborough, York, Gloucester, Lincoln and Bath were all virtually completely destroyed at one time or another.

■ ABOVE LEFT *A fire overwhelms a large building on the south side of the River Thames in eighteenth-century London.*

■ ABOVE RIGHT *A manual fire pump is put through its paces in this late seventeenth-century print.*

■ BELOW *Shouldering their manual pump, firemen dash to an urban fire in eighteenth-century Constantinople.*

The situation was no different in the other great cities of Europe, where the risk of frequent fire also drove the quest for better firefighting equipment. In the early sixteenth century, the Portuguese introduced some very large metal fire squirts, far bigger than any in use up to that time. Each one required a number of men to hold it while it was filled with water and then discharged on to a fire. In 1518, Anthony Blattner, a goldsmith of Augsburg, Germany, attempted to provide some reasonable mobility for a firefighting response by mounting a large fire squirt on a wheeled carriage. Most major cities of this time had

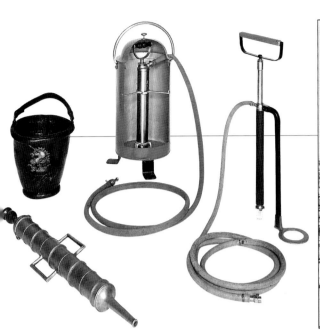

■ ABOVE LEFT *An old hand-pump and leather bucket once provided for the most effective firefighting effort.*

■ ABOVE RIGHT *A seventeenth-century German print of the Great Fire of London (1666) shows the enormous fire spread on the north bank of the Thames. By this time efforts were being made to create firebreaks at each end of the inferno.*

some system of fire squirts and bucket chains in place, which at best relied upon individuals and a few engineers with an interest in the subject to organize a firefighting effort in the event of a large fire.

It was the second Great Fire of London, which started in a baker's shop on 2 September 1666, that acted as a turning point, galvanizing efforts to move the science and practice of firefighting into a new age. The fire burned for four days and nights spreading in three directions before many unaffected buildings were deliberately demolished in its path to form an enormous firebreak. By the time it had subsided in its intensity, an area of almost two square miles of the City had been razed to the ground. Thirteen thousand homes, 84 churches and 44 livery halls lay in a smouldering ruin. More than 100,000 Londoners were made homeless and the fiscal damage was breath-taking, but, remarkably, only six people lost their lives. The direct aftermath of the Great Fire led to the first serious measures to provide organized fire brigades equipped to tackle fire, and the next 50 years were to see some major developments in public fire protection.

■ RIGHT *The sheer extent of the Great Fire of London was captured in oil by Waggoner. The widespread devastation provided the impetus for further development of effective firefighting.*

FIRE COMPANIES AND BRIGADES

As the aftermath of the Great Fire of London reverberated through Europe, everyone with an interest in fire extinction methods strove even harder to provide more effective means of tackling the threat of fire.

In 1673, a fire broke out in Amsterdam's Lijnbaan, (Ropewalk). As in the Great Fire, the flames spread with incredible rapidity through the back streets and passageways, engulfing many buildings. Some success was achieved in controlling the fire using innovative firefighting equipment designed by the Dutch engineer Van der Heiden. Fortunately for the city's population, he had a few years earlier invented a portable manual pump, which he attached to specially constructed leather hoses.

By the time of the Amsterdam fire, action was being taken in England to try to ensure that the enormous damage and upset of the Great Fire of London would never happen again. In 1680, Dr Nicholas Barbon initiated the world's first Fire Office, where customers could buy insurance and restitution cover against potential damage caused by fire. Barbon's enterprise soon failed, as there were simply too many claims to be met. Five years later a different type of scheme was set up when an insurance company created its own fire brigade to actively minimize the extent of fire damage and thus the size of a subsequent overall claim. It did this by mobilizing a band of firefighters drawn from the ranks of River Thames watermen in the event of a fire.

When in 1711 a conflagration in Boston destroyed over 100 buildings, North America suffered one of its largest fires to date. It burned for eight hours before coming under some control, causing 12 fatalities. The aftermath of this huge fire spurred Americans on to be more reactive to the risks of fire by

■ LEFT *Early pumps like this c.1680 manual fire engine could only provide an intermittent jet and were cumbersome and heavy. Water was poured into the central trough of the pump, and a pumping action on the two handles operated two plungers to produce a jet of water from the nozzle.*

developing firefighting equipment that was on a par with what was becoming available elsewhere in the world.

INSURANCE FIRE BRIGADE COMPANIES

In London good progress was being made, and by 1720, twelve different insurance fire brigade company schemes were in place. Each provided its firemen (watermen) with colourful uniforms to be worn when at a fire at an insured property. A company's firefighters

■ BELOW *The workings of an eighteenth-century two-man manual fire pump are shown in this French watercolour of the time. Before the use of air vessels, the efficiency of manual pumps depended entirely upon the speed and physical stamina of the pumpers.*

relied on metal firemarks fixed in a prominent position to the front-facing wall of a building to identify the insuring company. Competition among the insurance companies in this growing business sector was keen and got increasingly fierce as the number of insurance brigades started to multiply around 1725. It became the practice that if the first insurance firemen on the scene found that the property was not insured with their company, they would simply stand by and make no attempt to tackle the outbreak. Worse still, when the appropriate insurance company fire crew did turn up, the first crew would actively harass and obstruct the newly arrived firemen. It was a sure recipe for chaos and inefficiency, but one that was to prevail for almost a century.

Alongside the development of equipment, firefighting practice was slowly becoming better structured and organized. By 1733, Boston had a functioning volunteer fire department, and four years later New York

■ ABOVE *Metal firemarks were once fixed to the outside of insured properties. In the event of a fire, the appropriate fire brigade could clearly see that the property was entitled to benefit from its firefighting efforts.*

■ LEFT *Insurance company firemen were attired in resplendent livery. This fireman, standing by his manual fire pump, was employed by the Royal Exchange Fire Office c.1800.*

■ RIGHT *Two men could operate this early eighteenth-century Dutch four-man manual fire pump.*

boasted no fewer than 35 firefighters. In 1774, George Washington himself was instrumental in setting up a fire department.

At the same time, Napoleon Bonaparte was addressing France's growing need for fire protection. He instructed that a division of the French army should provide the manpower for a regular fire brigade to protect Paris and its inhabitants. The division was known as the Brigade de Sapeurs-Pompiers. By 1800, the Paris firefighting force possessed 30 powerful hand pumps to assist them in their task.

Early on in the nineteenth century, Britain's fire brigades were still manned by generally poorly organized and trained volunteer or part-time personnel. In 1824, however, after a series of serious fires, the city of Edinburgh, Scotland, made a momentous decision that would revolutionize firefighting everywhere. They amalgamated the various insurance brigades operating independently in the city to create Great Britain's first municipal fire brigade and called it the Edinburgh Fire Engine Establishment.

JAMES BRAIDWOOD

The Edinburgh city fathers duly appointed James Braidwood, a 24-year-old surveyor, to lead the new 80-strong volunteer corps. Braidwood wasted no time in training and preparing his firemen for the tasks ahead. He drilled them relentlessly day and night, working off ladders and on roofs, and getting water to normally inaccessible areas. Before long Edinburgh had the most effective firefighters in the land.

News of Braidwood's success soon spread to London where the cramped social housing conditions and industrial processes of the time combined to create an enormous risk of fire

■ **ABOVE LEFT** *In 1851, Frederick Hodges, the owner of a gin distillery, provided two horse-drawn manual fire engines to protect his company. Over the next decade, his company's firefighters attended hundreds of fires alongside London's regular brigade. This richly embellished Merryweather manual was presented to Hodges by grateful citizens in 1862.*

■ **ABOVE RIGHT** *James Braidwood, one of the fathers of modern firefighting, commanded the Edinburgh fire brigade from 1824 until he was invited, in 1832, to lead London's first professional fire brigade.*

■ **RIGHT** *Known as the Fire King, Eyre Massey Shaw led the London fire brigade for 25 years, from 1861, during which time he pioneered new firefighting techniques and equipment.*

and threat to life and property. By 1826, moves were afoot to merge London's principal insurance brigades into one effective force, and in 1832, Braidwood was invited to become Superintendent of the London Fire Engine Establishment (LFEE). Initially he had command of 80 full-time firefighters based at 19 stations across central London. Although Braidwood's new London brigade had to cover a population much larger than that of Edinburgh he was given the same number of

firemen as the Edinburgh force. This number grew significantly, however, as the fire cover response was steadily increased to include the wider area of Greater London.

Braidwood had gained extensive organizational experience in Edinburgh and immediately set about putting it to good use. He replaced the diverse uniforms of the firemen's former employers, issuing his men with practical black tunics and leather helmets and boots. He introduced a proper rank structure and a pension scheme. He also instigated a new and strict training routine that encouraged close quarters firefighting. This involved crews trying, where possible, to get inside a building on fire in order to tackle the flames at their seat. Until then, most firefighting efforts had involved aiming water jets through windows in an attempt to contain a fire, rather than a strategy of extinguishing flames at close quarters. In practice, however, it was not possible for firemen to stay inside burning buildings for long before the smoke and heat forced them out into fresh air.

The new chief also drilled his men in the dark, setting them to deal with imaginary fires, often in awkward and difficult locations, such as in attics and on rooftops. They had to work at height, off ladders and with hoses, until they were completely proficient. To keep his firemen alert and to ensure a speedy response to a real call-out, Braidwood would also 'turn out' fire stations on test calls at odd hours.

James Braidwood reigned supreme for almost the next 30 years as a world-leading authority in his field, but his life came to a tragic and sudden end on 22 June 1861, when a small fire broke out in a riverside warehouse just below Tower Bridge. Flames quickly spread through the narrow alleyways to become

■ RIGHT *A fireman of the London Fire Engine Establishment, c.1860, wears a recently issued uniform. Fire chief James Braidwood replaced the colourful, but impractical, insurance company uniforms with leather helmets, serge tunics and knee-length leather boots. The new style of fireman's uniform became the standard in Europe and elsewhere for the next hundred years or so.*

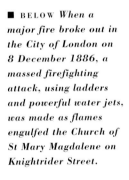

■ BELOW *When a major fire broke out in the City of London on 8 December 1886, a massed firefighting attack, using ladders and powerful water jets, was made as flames engulfed the Church of St Mary Magdalene on Knightrider Street.*

a huge conflagration. Characteristically leading his men from the front, Braidwood was killed when tons of masonry in the gable end of a building crashed down. His funeral cortege stretched for 2.5 kilometres/1½ miles and brought much of London to a halt.

SIR EYRE MASSEY SHAW

Braidwood was succeeded as London's fire chief by Captain (later Sir) Eyre Massey Shaw, an Irish army officer who had previously

commanded the joint Belfast police and fire brigade. For almost the next three decades, Shaw became the Western world's driving force in firefighting and fire safety. When, in 1866, the British Parliament set up the Metropolitan Fire Brigade, the forerunner of today's London Fire Brigade, Shaw commanded the largest professional fire brigade in the world. The brigade had already been expanded in the early 1860s to 59 fire stations and included many manual escape ladder stations, and Shaw introduced more improvements. He brought in steam-powered pumps, installed a telegraphic communication system and set up an intensive training regime for his firemen. Such was Shaw's expertise that he was in great demand. He crossed the Atlantic to review several American fire brigades and also advised Queen Victoria, in England, on fire safety in the royal palaces. In the 1870s the Prince of Wales, a keen amateur fireman, regularly attended large London fires in his company.

AMERICAN BRIGADES

There was a similar steady expansion in the provision of effective fire brigades in America, although early in the nineteenth century these were still mostly manned by volunteers. Nonetheless, an increasing number of serious outbreaks of fire threatened the economic and

■ ABOVE *The Great Fire of New York broke out on 16 December 1835. Explosives had to be used to create a firebreak before the huge blaze could be brought under control.*

■ BELOW *This double-decker horse-drawn fire engine would have been developed for use by fire companies.*

social fabric of the emerging nation. One such fire broke out in the infant business district of New York during a spell of extremely cold weather in December 1835. It started in an area of warehouses and shops, and the savage flames rapidly engulfed everything in their path. The severity of the ice and frost meant ready access to water supplies was difficult, and it was not until several buildings had been blown up to create a firebreak that the spreading inferno was eventually checked and subdued.

The end of the American Civil War saw the establishment of America's first professional fire brigade, in New York, and in 1865 it included 33 horse-drawn manually pumped engines, 11 ladders and 600 paid firemen. Not long after that, steam pumps came into widespread use in America.

Chicago suffered a devastating fire in 1871. It started in a timber mill and spread to destroy four blocks of buildings. As soon as this outbreak was brought under control after several hours, another fire started nearby, possibly ignited by sparks from the original

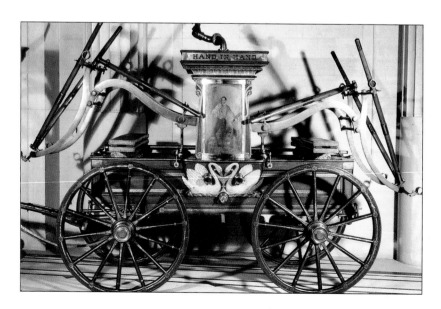

■ RIGHT *The Great Fire of Chicago broke out on 1 October 1871. It raged for 24 hours and extended over an area of 10 square kilometres/ 4 square miles.*

blaze. Fanned by a very strong wind, the second fire soon engulfed rows of timber properties and before long had become a conflagration. The strong wind rendered many firefighting jets useless, and the flames jumped across the river. Chicago fire crews, already weary from the first blaze, sent urgent telegraphic requests for help which brought crews from all around. The firefighting effort was also hampered by the thousands of Chicago's residents fleeing the advancing flames. The fire burned for 24 hours, before

coming under control with the assistance of heavy rain. More than 300 residents died in this terrible fire, which made 100,000 people homeless and destroyed over 18,000 buildings.

As a consequence of the Great Fire of Chicago, the strength of the city's fire department was doubled, and by 1876 it could muster 390 officers and men, 34 steam pumps, 150 horses, 26 sets of wheeled rescue ladders and approximately 11,000m/35,000ft of hose. Like many other progressive city brigades, Chicago was also installing street alarm boxes to speed up the call-out process.

The provision and development of fire brigades in different parts of the world did not follow any pattern, except that, unsurprisingly, those cities and towns that had suffered a devastating fire seem to have been the keenest to provide a well organized and equipped fire brigade. Many countries were quick to take up British and American developments in equipment and training. For example, in 1875 Sydney, Australia, could boast the most up-to-date British Merryweather steam pumps, whereas in Yokohama, Japan, firefighters had only just phased out wooden hand squirts that were truly of seventeenth-century origin.

■ BELOW *In this 1861 print, American fire crews are seen tackling a major fire with an assortment of manual fire engines.*

■ LEFT *To compensate for the shortage of firefighting vehicles in London at the beginning of World War II, taxicabs were pressed into service. This Austin carries some hose and a short ladder and tows a trailer pump.*

THE MODERN ERA

By the 20th century, most of the world's larger towns had made the provision of a regular municipal fire brigade. People understood that, apart from the constant threat to life, fire could have severe economic implications. In many areas, some of the financial cost of fire cover was beginning to be subsidized by both central and local government grants. In the smaller towns, however, volunteers continued to man the pumps and provide basic fire cover.

The major landmark in this period was the coming of the motorized fire engine, which enabled firefighters to respond more speedily to an incident and to carry with them an increasing amount of specialized firefighting and rescue equipment other than ladders and hose. The sheer power of firefighting water jets that came with motorized pumps was another improvement, and the first regular use of breathing sets and high aerial ladders meant that entire firefighting strategies could be more focused than in the past.

THE CHANGING WORLD

During the early and middle stages of the twentieth century, international conflict and war presented fire brigades with their biggest

■ LEFT *Fire crews of the Vienna Fire Brigade proudly pose with three pumps and a turntable ladder, c.1920. A bugler stands on a running board to warn of the vehicle's approach.*

challenges to date. World War I saw a number of Zeppelin airship bombing raids upon several British cities and towns. In 1915 one particular raid caused 29 separate fires in London, which severely damaged the City financial district. For the first time in history, firefighters found themselves in action as bombs fell; a number of men were injured during such a raid.

This incident would seem like nothing compared to the aerial bombing raids experienced by both British and German cities during World War II. British firefighters were the first to suffer the terrible aftermath of incendiary and high explosive raids when, in 1940, Germany's Luftwaffe targeted London and provincial centres. From September onwards, London was raided on 57 consecutive nights. The service took a terrible pounding, even though by then a government scheme to reinforce the 1,600 separate and individual professional fire brigades across Great Britain with 23,000 volunteers was in place. On some nights more than 2,000 pumps were in use in London. The ports and other strategic targets were also badly hit, and a convoy reinforcement scheme sent pumps to support local crews.

Firefighters were literally in the front line of battle, and the fire services on both sides of the conflict suffered heavy casualties, with many

■ ABOVE *Continual German bombardment during the London Blitz put the capital's firefighters under severe pressure. This view from the dome of St Paul's Cathedral shows the fire devastation on 30 December 1940.*

regular and auxiliary firefighters being killed or injured. From the early part of 1942 it was the turn of German firefighters to feel the strain when the Royal Air Force and the US Air Force took their intensive bombing campaign to German cities and armaments factories. Entire urban areas were set ablaze with incendiary and high-explosive bombs, giving fire crews on the ground little opportunity to restrict the severity of the flames.

The latter stages of the war saw the arrival of the German V-I Flying Bomb, followed by more devastating V-2 rockets. These fell in large numbers on London and south-east England in 1944–5, contributing to the tens of thousands of civilian casualties on both sides of the war. They also created new rescue challenges for firemen who had to assist in extricating people from beneath the debris of bombed buildings.

The British fire service was nationalized in order to standardize operational procedures and equipment during the war. Both sides pressed into service reserve government motor and trailer pumps and aerial ladders to supplement the normal firefighting strength. When peace came, it took the brigades almost a decade to recover. Under post-war economic conditions, fire engine and firefighting developments languished until the early 1950s, when a new generation of firefighting equipment began to emerge.

■ LEFT *In November 1943 a crew of Cologne firefighters tackle post air-strike flames with a meagre jet of water. Following intense attacks by Britain's RAF, German firefighters struggled with hundreds of fires.*

THE MODERN FIRE SERVICE

During the second half of the twentieth century the fire service developed at a steadily accelerating pace as it responded to a rapidly changing world. It embraced new technologies and materials as they were developed, while adapting to the continually evolving nature of firefighting and rescue work and an increasing incidence of emergencies.

The post-war age saw the introduction of better-quality domestic housing and a steady eradication of many traditional causes of fire in older dwellings, such as open fires, paraffin and oil stoves, and cramped cooking conditions. New properties incorporated fire protection within their structure and had better means of escape in case of fire. One innovation, for example, was the self-closing door designed to contain smoke within the affected part of the premises.

Yet, in spite of all these improvements, fire continued to be a threat. Modern homes contained a high level of flammable materials, including plastic and other man-made products such as foam fillings in furniture. When these were involved in fire they emitted considerable quantities of thick toxic smoke that could rapidly fill an entire dwelling with black,

choking fumes. Furthermore, they could easily be set alight by a carelessly discarded cigarette. Additionally, the widespread use of electricity and a growing number of domestic electrical appliances in the home gave rise to increasing incidences of fire caused by either malfunction or misuse.

Another cause of fire in the resurgence of industry after World War II was the development of new manufacturing methods, which often involved high temperatures, and the widespread growth of chemical use in the production of new synthetic materials. At the same time, many industrial factories and

■ ABOVE *Many brigades make use of fully crewed rescue helicopters, like this highly trained Japanese team based at Osaka.*

■ LEFT *US navy fire-fighters deal effectively with a modern-day chemical fire.*

■ BELOW *Equipped with breathing sets and heat-resistant clothing, American firefighters prepare to enter a burning building in Boston.*

■ BELOW *The fire service uniform differs from country to country but is recognizable the world over.*

■ BOTTOM *Regular training sessions prepare modern firefighters for every eventuality. Here, a firefighter gets to work dealing with a burning fuel tanker.*

companies were located in old buildings, few of which were laid out with fire precautions and the safety of the workforce in mind.

In the wake of several major fatal fires in the 1950s, in industrial and other premises where fire precautions had been woefully inadequate, British authorities introduced fire-prevention legislation, and a number of the new laws were enacted. Higher levels of fire safety were required in petrol stations following a fire that caused 11 deaths in Bristol, in 1951; in factory premises after a fire in a West Yorkshire woollen mill in 1956, which directly caused eight deaths; in department stores after 11 shoppers died in Liverpool in 1960; and in licensed club premises following 19 fatalities in Lancashire in 1961. Similar legislation followed fatal fires in hotels, hostels and homes for the elderly. Other countries experiencing similar tragedies introduced fire legislation.

Another increasing cause of fire in modern society is arson, whether motivated by criminal intent or insurance fraud purposes. To combat this trend, modern brigades employ trained anti-arson marshals and fire investigation teams. Working closely with law-enforcement agencies, they combine forensic skills with sophisticated equipment.

CURRENT PRACTICE
Today, various local authorities provide a 24-hour firefighting service that can respond swiftly to an alarm call to any fire or emergency.

■ ABOVE *In some firefighting situations, aluminized heat-resistant suits and hoods are worn to protect against extreme heat exposure.*

A critical part of modern fire brigade operation is the control or despatch centre, which handles all incoming fire and emergency calls and mobilizes response. These centres are staffed 24 hours a day by specialist uniformed personnel who, having despatched fire engines to the scene of an incident, will control all subsequent radio traffic, despatch reinforcements as necessary and generally monitor the progress of operations. In addition to attending emergencies, fire brigades contribute to general fire safety in other ways. They apply fire-prevention legislation and educate the public about general fire safety and awareness through visits to schools, youth groups, retirement homes and hospitals.

Modern firemen are trained to use a wide range of equipment and in the latest firefighting techniques, which involve tackling fires at close quarters inside a burning building. To cope with such adverse conditions as extreme heat, high levels of thick smoke and

■ LEFT *Thermal imaging cameras enable firefighters to see through smoke to locate casualties and the seat of a fire. This ISG Talisman Spirit is a new generation of miniature infra-red firefighting cameras.*

■ RIGHT *A dramatic live fire test puts an aluminized firefighting suit through its paces.*

■ LEFT *Firefighters have removed part of a thatch in order to create a firebreak that will prevent flames spreading along the entire length of the roof.*

whatever small fire was burning. Early firefighting efforts also often attempted to remove the material source of the fire from the flames by creating a firebreak – perhaps pulling down a thatched roof in the direct path of the fire, or by the more drastic method of using gunpowder to demolish an entire building. Modern firefighting methods are, thankfully, more sophisticated although water is generally still the most commonly used extinguishing medium the world over. Water readily provides an immediate cooling effect, particularly when applied at high pressure and in fine atomized particles known as water fog. This lowers the ignition source below the temperature at which the combustion process can take place.

humidity, their equipment includes a personal breathing set and a flash-proof firefighting kit that enables them to get close to the seat of the fire. Technical aids such as thermal-imaging cameras, which see through smoke, and personal radios further allow modern firefighters to deal with fires and save lives more successfully than ever.

The whole basis of successful modern-day firefighting is to remove one or more of the three constituents of fire in order to extinguish a blaze. In ancient times, a water bucket chain probably only had a modest effect in cooling

■ BELOW LEFT *Boston Fire Department crews enter the upper floors of a burning building from massed ladders.*

■ BELOW RIGHT *A prompt attack with an extinguisher prevents a small fire from escalating.*

SPECIALIST INCIDENTS

Some types of fire, however, demand the use of special techniques. Large oil and petroleum fires require the oxygen supply to be cut off from the flames on the surface of the burning liquid. This is done by applying foam to the burning surface, so starving the fire of the oxygen it needs. A fire that involves chemicals also needs special attention, requiring the application of dry powder to exclude oxygen from the combustion process. Firefighters also need to take great care when tackling electrical fires. Water cannot be applied to such fires due to the risk of electrocution, via the conduction of the current through water. Instead dry powder or inert gas must be used to exclude the oxygen from the surface of burning electrical components such as cabling, switch gear, computers and televisions.

■ TOP *A major fire at a plastics plant in Cleveland, England, produces a huge cloud of toxic smoke.*

■ ABOVE *This Sides 6x6 foam tender is in service at Charles de Gaulle Airport, Paris.*

■ ABOVE RIGHT *Firefighting in winter is hindered by freezing snow, fog and ice.*

■ RIGHT *In an attempt to combat the rise in the number of arson fires during 2001, the London Fire Brigade introduced sniffer dogs as part of their fire investigation teams.*

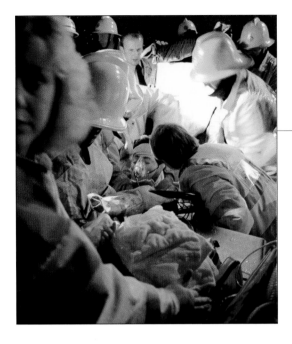

In addition to the urban and rural fire brigades that cover the needs of the general population and most industry, specialist fire brigades now exist to serve particular fire and emergency risks. Large airports, for example, are required to provide their own professional fire and rescue service, which has to be equipped and trained to deal with a possible aircraft fire or crash where large quantities of burning fuel might be involved. Airport fire engines must therefore have a large foam capacity and a cross-country all-wheel drive, and also carry specialist cutting tools. Similarly, on-site industrial fire brigades that protect large petrochemical complexes also need sufficient quantities of water, foam and dry powder to deal with large-scale outbreaks of fire where flammable liquids or gases will be burning or pose an explosive threat.

Due to the nature of their high-level training and up-to-date equipment, firefighters are able to tackle a wide range of emergencies, and a significant number of emergency call-outs are of a non-fire nature, many involving life-or-death situations. Road traffic accidents, especially on motorways and other highway networks, have grown dramatically since the 1950s with our increased dependence on cars. As people are often trapped in their crushed vehicles, the fire service has progressively

■ ABOVE LEFT *Fire brigades increasingly attend non-fire emergencies such as road crashes.*

■ ABOVE RIGHT *Firefighters work to release the driver of a car that has collided with a tram in central Manchester, England.*

■ BELOW *Fireboats are essential firefighting equipment for busy ports and harbours. They pump their jets directly from the water beneath them.*

refined its expertise in dealing with such difficult situations. Other non-fire emergencies include gas explosions, leaking or spilled toxic and hazardous chemicals, machinery accidents, and people or animals trapped in various predicaments. The effects of a range of extreme weather conditions can also greatly increase firefighters' workloads. Incidents such as storm-force winds, lightning strikes and flooding after severe rain or thaw all place a huge demand on firefighters. In some countries they are also called on to deal with the effects of natural disasters, such as volcanic eruptions and earthquakes.

Fire Engine Development

Modern fire engines are some of the most high-profile vehicles on the road. They have come a long way since the first simple attempts in the seventeenth century to mount a manually pumped machine on wheels so that it could be pulled or pushed to the scene of a fire. The subsequent arrival of steam and then electric battery-powered fire pumps each heralded a new era for fire engine development as new engineering ideas and practice provided progressively more powerful vehicles for the world's fire brigades. With the coming of the motor age, fire engine design burgeoned as a prolific number of international manufacturers came on the scene. Today a wide range of pumps, aerial ladders, platforms and many other specialist fire engines are in use all around the world.

MANUAL PUMPS

The latter part of the seventeenth century was a landmark time for the development of the early manually pumped, wheeled fire engine. Prior to this time, pumps were carried to the scene of the fire by firemen, but the regular occurrence of serious fires at that time added purpose to the quest for more powerful and efficient fire engines as well as for ancillary equipment to assist in the battle against the flames.

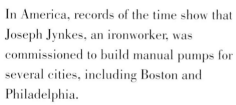

■ LEFT *Dating from around 1800, this manual fire engine saw service at the Woolwich Arsenal Ordnance Military Depot, in south-east London.*

EARLY DEVELOPMENTS

During this period various serious attempts were made to produce a reliable wheeled pump that could throw a powerful water jet on to a fire. The early pumps were basically glorified large squirts or syringes with a single-cylinder barrel that drew water in on the upward stroke of the plunger and discharged the contents on the downward stroke. A number of these manually pumped fire engines were described by the English author John Bate in his *Treatise on Art and Nature* (1634).

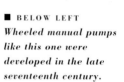

■ BELOW LEFT *Wheeled manual pumps like this one were developed in the late seventeenth century.*

■ BELOW RIGHT *Pump pioneer Richard Newsham's first manual fire engine of 1734 used an air reservoir to produce a continuous water jet.*

In America, records of the time show that Joseph Jynkes, an ironworker, was commissioned to build manual pumps for several cities, including Boston and Philadelphia.

In 1655, a German named Hans Hautch was the first engineer to incorporate an air-vessel in a manual pump. This used air stored in a copper cylinder to ensure a steady and constant firefighting stream of water. Then in 1673, Dutchman Jan Van der Heiden, a pioneer of firefighting engineering, success-fully manufactured the first leather hose. It was constructed of 15m/50ft lengths of sewn leather fitted with brass screw couplings at each end. Once screwed together, this hose allowed water to be pumped over a short distance, dispensing

with the need for labour-intensive bucket chains and allowing firefighters to discharge water at close range on to a fire as it was being pumped manually. Van der Heiden also mounted his manual pumps on to sleds so that they could be transported down to the Amsterdam canal sides in order to maximize the available water supply. Van der Heiden's pumps and hose were successfully used in combination for the first time in 1673, to combat a serious fire that broke out in the Amsterdam Ropewalk.

Then, in 1721, Richard Newsham, a London button manufacturer with a keen interest in all things mechanical, turned his attention to improving the design of manual fire pumps. He produced a pump that depended on a clever system of levers, chain-operated pistons and air reservoirs, and outperformed everything else on the scene. The use of air resevoirs produced a constant firefighting water jet, providing that the water supply via a bucket chain or hose line did not fail.

By 1725, Newsham's largest manual pumps each required up to 14 volunteer 'pumpers' to work the long handles, one on each side of the pump. These large manual pumps were able to project a water jet as far as 50m/165ft and discharge about 727 litres/160 gallons per minute. Many were commissioned by the emerging insurance companies of that time, but there was as yet no apparent government support or encouragement. Newsham's successful engineering principles were soon being adapted and copied by fire engineers all over Europe and North America.

■ ABOVE *This c.1735 wheeled Merryweather compact manual pump carried leather hose. This pump was made almost 60 years after the leather hose was developed.*

■ BELOW *Richard Mason of Philadelphia built this wheeled manual pump c.1792.*

By the beginning of the nineteenth century, the development of manual fire engines in America started to match the pace in England. American manual fire-engine makers of the time included William Hunneman, James Smith, Patrick Lyon, John Rodgers, and Button and Company. Among their designs were powerful 'double-deckers', with one line of pumpers standing on the fire engine while a second line worked pump handles at street level.

Manual pump designs continued to be improved until well into the nineteenth century, but their output was directly proportional to the physical effort imparted at the pumping levers. In effect they were limited by the number of volunteer pumpers prepared to provide the sustained physical effort required to produce an effective and continuous jet of water. Pumping teams were proud of their strength and stamina and often took part in competitions. Such contests were held at London's Great Exhibition, in 1851, and at a similar event in Paris. in 1855.

HORSE POWER

A further improvement in firefighting came when manual pumps were mounted on horse-drawn chassis. Apart from increased mobility and response speed, this development also meant that manufacturers could produce heavier and more powerful pumping units. Better design, stronger metal components and more robust pumping mechanisms combined to keep manual fire engine development moving forward at a steady pace.

HORSE POWER PIONEERS

In the United States, Patrick Lyon led the move towards horse power. In Britain, Richard Newsham had already mounted some of his heavier pumps on a horse-drawn chassis early in the eighteenth century, and by 1820 most effective manuals were horse drawn, with companies such as London-based Merryweather & Sons, and W. J. Tilley (subsequently Shand Mason & Co) leading the way.

Horse power meant that for the first time firemen could ride on the fire engine itself, and before long manufacturers provided footboards along each side of the manual pump's

■ ABOVE *Horse-drawn vehicles, carrying pumps and men, speeded up response to a fire.*

■ BELOW *This model 1881 Merryweather manual fire engine carried a toolbox on which the firemen sat as they were transported at speed to the fire.*

bodywork behind the driver, or coachman as he was often called. Handrails were also added so that the crew could hang on as the fire engine was galloped at some speed to the outbreak of fire. The crew member immediately behind the coachman remained standing in order to operate a long brake lever that stopped the rear wheels under the shouted direction of the coachman.

As adaptations were made to carry small ladders and secure a few lengths of leather hose and some brass nozzles, the horse-drawn manual pumps developed into the first self-contained fire engines. Travelling at speeds of up to 30 kilometres/20 miles per hour, horse power meant that firefighters arrived at a fire outbreak much more quickly than before, and without being exhausted from the physical effort of pulling a heavy pump.

In 1851, Merryweather produced a very successful standard horse-drawn vehicle, designed mostly around the

particular requirements of London's Fire
Engine Establishment. The pump had two
vertical single-acting cylinders driven by links
from the outside pump handles, and a large
in-built copper air vessel to ensure a constant
discharge of water. The wooden body and frame
was spring-mounted on large road wheels fitted
with brakes and designed to be drawn by two
horses. The bodywork incorporated several
lockers for hose and other fittings. This model
continued to be manufactured, both for use in
Great Britain and for export, until steam power
eventually supplanted the manually operated
fire engine. In rural areas and on country
estates, however, 'manuals' continued to be
used for some years into the twentieth century.

The new vehicles depended on horses being
available when a fire call came in. In rural
areas, few brigades were busy enough to justify
keeping horses, so arrangements would be
made to use the nearest suitable horses to the
fire station. In large cities, however, where call-
outs were frequent, many brigades acquired
their own horses to speed up turnout.

■ ABOVE *In the past,
stately homes and
country estates, like
industry, might have
owned their own fire
engine, such as this
c.1866 horse-drawn
manual pump.*

■ BELOW LEFT *In
the late nineteenth
century, busy fire
brigades bred and kept
their own horses at
brigade headquarters.*

■ BELOW RIGHT *A
later innovation of the
horse-drawn fire engine
was to carry ladders
and equipment, as well
as men, to the scene
of the fire.*

The best fire horses were bred to combine
strength and speed. They were cared for at the
fire station in purpose-built stalls close to the
fire engine itself. All the fire horses of
London's Metropolitan Fire Brigade were
eventually descended from a single line of
greys specially bred for stamina, controllability
in the noise and bustle of a busy city throng,
and their ability to remain calm.

Horse-drawn fire engines had no warning
devices such as the penetrating bells, horns
and electronic wailers we are accustomed to on
modern vehicles. Instead, once they had turned
out for a fire, the entire crew would
continuously shout out 'Hi! Hi!' to alert road
users and the general public of their impending
high-speed approach.

THE AGE OF STEAM

Steam power was first successfully applied to a firefighting pump in 1829, thereby revolutionizing the service. Fire brigades no longer had to rely on a team of straining volunteers to get a decent firefighting jet of water. They simply let the steam drive the powerful jets of water for them.

BRAITHWAITE AND ERICSSON

The world's first steam-driven fire pump was the combined work of two London-based engineers, George Braithwaite and John Ericsson. Their 10hp, 2-cylinder steam engine drove a 2-cylinder fire pump that, like the later manual pumps, utilized a large-capacity air vessel to ensure a continuous firefighting flow of water through leather hoses to the nozzles.

The pump on Braithwaite and Ericsson's fire engine was mounted at the front of a horse-drawn chassis, behind the coachman's seat.

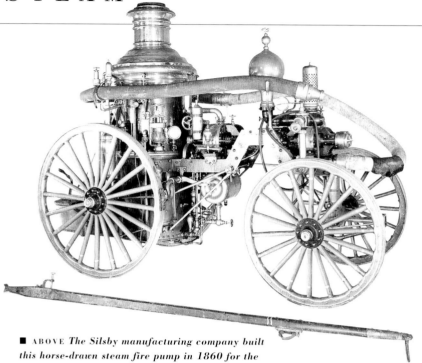

■ ABOVE *The Silsby manufacturing company built this horse-drawn steam fire pump in 1860 for the Philadelphia Fire Department, Pennsylvania, USA.*

■ BELOW *The first American steam-driven fire engine was constructed by Paul Hodge. It had to be jacked up to allow the rear wheels to rotate as flywheels.*

The pump's steam engine had an under-slung firebox fed with coke through a fire-hole door at the rear of the fire engine. The twin pistons of the steam pump were connected directly to the plungers of the fire pump. The boiler took about 13 minutes to reach full working steam pressure and once the fire engine had a full head of steam it could produce enough pressure to project a jet of water 27m/90ft high at approximately 680 litres/150 gallons per minute. The whole fire engine weighed 2¼ tons.

During the height of the cold winter of 1830, Braithwaite and Ericsson's revolutionary fire engine attended a serious fire in a theatre in the Soho district of London. It pumped water continuously into the building for five hours, long before which all the manual pumps of the London Fire Engine Establishment had frozen.

RESISTANCE TO CHANGE
Surprisingly perhaps, steam power was rather slow to catch on in London. For one thing, many of the volunteers who manned the pumps were reluctant to lose their 'pumping' payment as well as the generous provision of beer that was traditionally served to replace the sweat lost through their physical effort. There was also fear of using the new technology for

■ ABOVE LEFT *Torrent, built by Merryweather (1863), was one of the earliest horse-drawn steam fire engines.*

■ ABOVE RIGHT *With their steam pump at the ready, these c.1900 firemen are ready to confront a fire.*

■ BELOW *A Victorian steamer is connected to a water main.*

pumping firefighting water. Even though steam engines had been safely used in British mines for some time, the power of steam was awesome and machines had been known to go wrong.

After the success of their first steam pump, Braithwaite and Ericsson constructed four similar fire engines. One of these was a 5hp single-cylinder model capable of throwing a jet of water over a distance of 30m/100ft that saw service in both Russia and France. The other three went to Liverpool and Berlin.

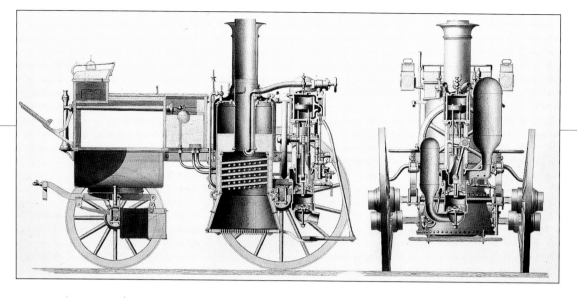

■ LEFT *These sectional drawings of an 1876 Shand Mason horse-drawn steam-powered fire pump show the engineering detail of the time. Shand Mason produced single and 2-cylinder pumps.*

Another factor in Britain's slow uptake of steam-powered fire pumps was concern that the sheer force of the water jets might cause additional damage to a building's structure. James Braidwood, the Superintendent of the London Fire Engine Establishment, personally resisted the introduction of steam power for over 25 years before he was killed at the huge 1861 Tooley Street conflagration. It was left to his successor, Captain Eyre Massey Shaw, to order the first 'steamers' for London's brigade, in 1863, and so begin the belated transition to steam power of one of the world's leading fire brigades.

DEVELOPMENTS IN STEAM POWER

There was no such reticence to adopt steam-powered fire pumps elsewhere. Paul Hodge, a New York engineer, constructed the first American-built steam-powered fire engine in 1840. Designed along the lines of an early railway locomotive, it was the world's first self-propelled fire engine, but it could also be hauled manually or by a pair of horses. When in use at a fire, the large rear wheels were jacked up off the ground so that they could act as large flywheels for the fire pump motion.

Other American steam pump designs soon followed. In 1851, William Lay of Philadelphia unveiled another self-propelled model. This was one of the first fire pumps to use a rotary pump able to throw 1800 litres/400 gallons of

water per minute. Over the next ten years, American interest in steam-powered fire engines continued at a high level. Horse-drawn models were produced independently by Alexander Latta, Abel Shawk and Lee & Lanard, and soon companies such as Button, Silsby, Clapp & Jones, Gleason & Bailey, and Rumsey & Co became major manufacturers, producing new machines for many years.

By the early 1860s the two principal steam fire engine manufacturers for Britain and Europe were Shand Mason & Co and Merryweather & Sons, London-based firms who remained fierce competitors for over half a century. Shand Mason produced their first steamer, pulled by a team of three horses instead of the usual two, in 1858. Three years later Merryweather produced their first steamer, named the Deluge. With its

■ BELOW *American LaFrance built this steam fire pump in 1896 for the Lynn, Massachusetts, Fire Department.*

■ ABOVE LEFT *The Amoskeag Company constructed this steam fire pump for the Lawrence, Massachusetts, Fire Department.*

■ ABOVE RIGHT *Many American steamers were heavier than British versions and needed to be drawn by three horses. This Amoskeag of New Haven, Connecticut, is a dramatic sight with smoke pouring from the boiler chimney.*

30-horsepower engine, it was probably the most powerful steam-powered fire pump built to date and was able to project a water jet to a height of 43m/140ft with a lateral throw of 65m/215ft. The two companies went on to produce both single and 2-cylinder models, Shand Mason preferring short-stroke high-revolution engines.

At fire stations, steam pumps were always kept ready for action, with the firebox carefully laid with kindling material and coal/coke so that it could be lit as the fire engine turned out. In later years, gas rings were lit under the boiler to warm the water inside. The air flow through the firebox during the dash to the fire would cause the fire to burn through so that on

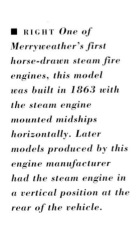

■ RIGHT *One of Merryweather's first horse-drawn steam fire engines, this model was built in 1863 with the steam engine mounted midships horizontally. Later models produced by this engine manufacturer had the steam engine in a vertical position at the rear of the vehicle.*

arrival at the incident, steam had usually been raised ready to power the fire pump. The mechanical care of the engine was normally the responsibility of a fireman-engineer on the crew who, once at the fire, would tend the fire and boiler water levels, and lubricate the reciprocating parts of the steam engine. In practice, providing there was a good supply of boiler water, coal or coke, and lubricating oil, the engine would keep on pumping indefinitely.

■ ABOVE *The 'crew' of a preserved Shand Mason steamer take part in a display staged at a fire engine rally.*

FIRE ENGINE TRIALS

As steam power became accepted, fire engine trials were regularly staged to give manufacturers the chance to show off the capabilities of their machines before large audiences of fire officers, government officials and the press. One of the largest such gatherings took place in London's Hyde Park as part of the 1861 International Exhibition. The event was so successful that another was staged in London two years later. There were ten entries for this second event, seven from Britain and three from America. Although all the steam pumps appeared to perform well and entertained the large crowds, the competition's outcome was difficult to gauge as complaints were made against the judges' lack of impartiality and their methods of assessment. Against all this publicity, steamer fire engines were coming into widespread use in the

professional brigades around the world. In 1864, Shand Mason delivered steam pumps for brigades as far apart as London, Russia, Bombay, New Zealand, Poland, Denmark, Ireland and Lisbon. Manual pumps remained in cities as reserve fire engines for another 30 years and continued to operate in many rural areas well into the twentieth century.

Although the development in the United States of steam pumps had heralded the construction there of the first self-propelled steamer fire engine in 1840, horse-drawn steam pumps continued to be made. Indeed, for the next three decades the focus was on developing horse-drawn steam pumps, which performed reliably and for long duration at fires. By the 1870s several manufacturers had started to produce effective self-propelled steam pumps in which the boiler steam also powered a propulsion engine driving the rear wheels.

■ RIGHT *This scale model of a Shand Mason steamer, seen from the rear, gleams with beautiful engineering. The original c.1880 fire engine was used by the Metropolitan Fire Brigade.*

■ RIGHT *This powerful 2-cylinder Merryweather steam fire pump was delivered new to Southgate Fire Brigade, north London, in 1894. It represented the zenith of British steam fire-engine power and efficiency.*

■ BELOW *The self-propelled Merryweather Fire King steam fire engine was introduced in 1899. It was a powerful pumping unit and capable of good speed, but its braking system left something to be desired.*

MANUFACTURING RIVALS

The Amoskeag firm had, in fact, been producing some large self-propelled steam fire engines for US fire departments since 1867. One of the company's biggest models, claimed to be the largest fire engine in the world, was supplied to Hartford Fire Department, Connecticut, in 1894. Weighing over 7 tons,

it could reach speeds of 48 kilometres/30 miles per hour and was reputed to have been capable of pumping a firefighting jet of water an incredible 107m/350ft into the air.

This American activity eventually spurred British manufacturer Merryweather, still the predominant European manufacturer of horse-drawn steam fire engines of the time, into action. In 1899, Merryweather produced a chain-driven self-propelled model called the Fire King. It weighed a hefty 5½ tons and was capable of a speed of 40 kilometres/25 miles per hour. It could also pump 1800 litres/400 gallons per minute, making it one of the most powerful fire engines of its time. This fire engine was subsequently exported worldwide.

The British Fire King and the American Amoskeag self-propelled steam fire engine suffered from their massive weight and were notoriously difficult to steer. Another problem was that the braking systems of both were incapable of efficiently halting such a mass. By the turn of the twentieth century, the era of the steam-powered fire engine, both horse-drawn and self-propelled, was coming to an end.

MOTORIZED POWER

The coming of the petrol-powered internal-combustion engine heralded a major step forward in the design and functional style of fire engines, and in the way firefighters tackled fires. More powerful fire engines were made possible, which could carry a growing variety of firefighting and rescue equipment. An innovative feature was a built-in water tank that fed powerful pumps driven directly from the road engine. This meant that for the first time in history fire crews had a firefighting water jet at their disposal on arrival at a fire, and gone were the days when crucial minutes were lost searching out a nearby water supply before anyone could tackle the flames. Motorized fire engines also gave fire brigades greater mobility, and faster response times.

ELECTRIC FIRE ENGINES

Before the widespread adoption of petrol-powered vehicles, a number of the larger professional fire brigades experimented with battery-powered electric fire engines. These were popular for a brief period from about 1905 but were extremely heavy due to the large number of lead-acid batteries needed to provide power to the electric motors. The other drawback was the fact that the batteries required frequent charging on mains electricity.

■ ABOVE *The first self-propelled car used by the Metropolitan (London) Fire Brigade was a Stanley steamer acquired in 1903 for the chief fire officer.*

■ LEFT *Lisbon Fire Brigade bought some state-of-the-art equipment when it acquired this 1913 Delahaye pump.*

■ RIGHT *Battery-driven electric vehicles like this Cedes pump and escape carrier were short-lived novelties at the start of the twentieth century.*

■ BELOW *London-based Merryweather produced this electric fire engine around 1905. The limited power capacity of the vehicle's batteries, together with their heavy weight, rendered the production shortlived. This view shows the crew preparing a hose line to work up a ladder at first floor level.*

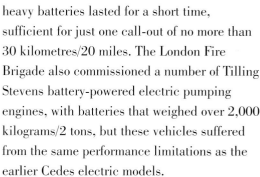

These appliances were pioneered by the French Cedes Company in conjunction with Daimler Motors of Austria, and a number went into service. Large batteries housed under the vehicle bonnet drove an electric motor mounted on the rear axle. At that time the heavy batteries lasted for a short time, sufficient for just one call-out of no more than 30 kilometres/20 miles. The London Fire Brigade also commissioned a number of Tilling Stevens battery-powered electric pumping engines, with batteries that weighed over 2,000 kilograms/2 tons, but these vehicles suffered from the same performance limitations as the earlier Cedes electric models.

Another disadvantage of electric engines was that their restricted battery power meant that the fire pump had to be driven by other means. Several designs soon appeared. One such, a cumbersome chemical apparatus resembling a large fire extinguisher, was carried on the rear of the electric vehicles. A chemical reaction expelled the contents of the water tank through hoses to the fire. Some engineers and fire brigades, such as in Hamburg in 1909, mounted an old steam plant on the battery-electric fire engine to provide the firefighting means. Even more adventurous was the action of the Hanover brigade, who in 1911 fitted an independent petrol-driven fire pump on the back of an electric road chassis.

THE DEVELOPMENT OF PETROL POWER

Several attempts were made to build an internal-combustion-engine fire vehicle at the turn of the twentieth century. They were virtually all based on an early car chassis and

often ended up as a run-around vehicle for the brigade's chief officer. In 1903, the Tottenham Brigade in north London took delivery of the world's first true petrol-engine fire engine – a new Merryweather model. Powered by a 24hp Aster petrol engine, it was designed to carry a 15m/50ft wheeled escape ladder. It also incorporated a small 'first-aid' water tank and hose reels actuated by chemical action. Tottenham's new Merryweather was located at Haringey, where a modern fire station had just been constructed.

THE FIRST PETROL FIRE ENGINES

One year later, in 1904, the first petrol fire engine to have an in-built fire pump driven off the road engine was manufactured for the Finchley Fire Brigade, in Middlesex, England. The decision to order the new petrol fire engine was largely due to the difficulty the Brigade was experiencing in obtaining suitable horses to pull its steamer. Many small brigades such as Finchley could not justify the cost of horses standing by in the station's stables, so had an informal arrangement with a local brewery or other business to borrow horses in the event of a call-out. During 1903 there had been several cases when Finchley Brigade had to wait up to 30 minutes for horses. In addition, poor mains water pressure in the area fuelled the fear that any major fire could not be adequately dealt with and would wreak havoc on life or property.

The Finchley Brigade's new vehicle was truly groundbreaking, partly due to its design, which had resulted from a careful collaboration between Chief Officer Sly and Merryweather's engineers. Powered initially by a 30hp Aster 4-cylinder engine driving twin rear wheels via

■ BELOW *A chain-driven Delahaye pump and hook
ladder tender of the Paris Fire Brigade, c.1920,
transports a complete fire crew. The rolled hose drum
mounted beneath the driving position is removable at
the scene of a fire.*

■ BELOW *A 1924
model Ahrens Fox
heavy pumper with its
characteristic front-
mounted pump.*

a chain drive, the engine was capable of a
steady 30 kilometres/20 miles per hour on the
road. It was later fitted with a 50hp motor to
improve its road speed. The petrol engine also
powered the 1136 litres/250 gallons per minute
reciprocating fire pump that fed hoses from two
delivery outlets at the sides of the fire engine.

The six-man crew had to stand on footboards
on each side of the vehicle during transit.

Finchley's new fire engine was also radical
in the equipment it carried – a three-section
ladder, portable fire extinguishers and a
272 litre/60 gallon water tank that supplied the
main fire pump. There was also a hose reel
supplied by a chemical action apparatus. This
fire engine was the forerunner of today's multi-
purpose fire engines, which are able to pump
water and carry a large range of firefighting and
rescue tools and associated equipment. The
historic Finchley fire engine is permanently on
view in London's Science Museum.

At this time in both the United States and
Europe, work was going on to produce a
reliable petrol-engine fire vehicle that could
provide power to both the engine and a built-in
fire pump. In 1906, Waterous, an American
manufacturer, went a step further when the
company unveiled a two-engine fire truck –

one engine to drive the road wheels and another to power the fire pump. Everything was considered, and there were even instances during the early twentieth century when horses were being used to pull carriage-mounted petrol-engine fire pumps. Several American companies produced fire vehicles constructed with a petrol-engine tractor unit that pulled a steam-driven fire pump behind.

Across the United States, names that would grace the motor fire-apparatus field for many years were beginning to emerge, including Mack, American LaFrance, Pirsch, Seagrave, and Ahrens-Fox. By the outbreak of World War I, Dennis was beginning to dominate much of the fire engine market in the UK and around the British Empire, although Leyland, Bedford, Albion, Commer and Merryweather all

■ ABOVE LEFT *London Fire Brigade introduced this Leyland foam tender, in 1910, for firefighting at petrol and oil installations.*

■ ABOVE RIGHT *In the 1920s the Paris Fire Brigade maintained a cine film unit to record its firefighting work in the French capital. The unit was mounted on a motor cycle and sidecar chassis.*

■ BELOW *Early American Ford pumpers, like this 1927 model, had brakes on the rear wheels only.*

produced fire engines of various types in significant numbers. Elsewhere, French car manufacturer Delahaye turned their hand to producing fire engines, and by the 1920s, Fiat (Italy and Austria), Isotta-Franchini (Italy), and Magirus and Metz (Germany) were among the growing number of international fire engine manufacturers.

DESIGN IMPROVEMENTS

This was a time of growing technical improvement in fire engine design, with many manufacturers looking seriously at the precise needs of firefighting pumps rather than relying on adapting existing commercial vehicles in their range. Twin rear wheels, the use of pneumatic tyres, and power-assisted brakes on all axles are examples of this trend.

By the 1930s, fire engines fell into three broad types. The most numerous were the general workhorse vehicles that delivered firefighting water and carried a variety of general firefighting equipment in their lockers. Second, came aerial turntable ladders, by then reaching up to 30m/100ft. Third, was a steadily growing group of specialized fire engines, which included dedicated foam tenders and hose layers.

Until now fire engines had been open, and in most parts of the world were fitted with transverse seating for the crew. British fire engine design still saw firemen clinging to outside-facing seats while getting rigged in their firefighting uniforms. This particular British fire-engine body style was known as the 'Braidwood' (after James Braidwood, the

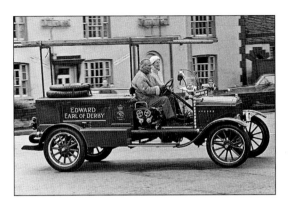

■ ABOVE LEFT *The Ford Model T British fire tender, c.1912, had a transverse-mounted fire pump beneath the driving position with two hose deliveries on each side of the vehicle.*

■ ABOVE RIGHT *This Dennis c.1933 G-type pump has a rear-mounted 1600 litres/350 gallons per minute pump.*

nineteenth-century reformer of fire brigades in Edinburgh and London). At this time several deaths and injuries resulted when crew were flung off a Braidwood-bodied fire engine on its way to a fire, often as it negotiated a sharp turn. As a direct result, several new models were introduced, notably that of Dennis, where the crew seating was provided in the vehicle's bodywork. Not to be outdone, in 1935 Leyland introduced the first totally enclosed limousine pumping fire engine, which set new standards of safety and comfort from the fire crew.

During the 1930s the diesel-powered engine started to appear in fire vehicles.

Austrian manufacturer Perl AG installed a 50hp diesel unit in several pumping fire engines for the Vienna city brigade. In Germany, Mercedes Benz began to use powerful 4.8 litre diesel engine units for fire service applications. At the same time petrol-powered engines were developed to extract more power, particularly in America, to meet the pumping needs of firefighters faced with ever higher tower blocks. As early as 1931 American LaFrance had produced a 12-cylinder V12 petrol engine that produced 240hp, enough to power fire pumps to produce 6,810 litres/1,500 gallons of firefighting water per minute.

■ RIGHT *In 1935, the British company Dennis delivered a number of the new Big Six models to London Fire Brigade's own specification. They had a rear-mounted 2250 litres/500 gallons per minute pump and carried a 15m/50ft wooden-wheeled escape ladder. The bodywork incorporated two rows of transverse seats for the crew.*

MODERN FIRE ENGINES

With the storm clouds of war gathering over Europe, fire brigades on both sides of the conflict were faced with the enormous and protracted task of fighting fires that might result from relentless bombing raids. As more nations became embroiled in the war, fire engine development, along with most other engineering and economic activity, suffered dramatically. Even though the countries involved slowly emerged into the post-war period of recovery and rebuilding, it was not until the early 1950s that fire engine design picked up once again.

By the outbreak of war in September 1939, the British government had bolstered its regular firefighting force of 20,000 with some 23,000 volunteer auxiliaries up and down the country equipped with several types of utility fire engine for the perceived tasks ahead. Among these appliances were Austin and Fordson heavy pumping units and trailer pumps towed behind a variety of requisitioned vehicles, which in London included black taxicabs. Several 30m/100ft Leyland/

■ ABOVE *This 1949 Kenworth HG721 heavy pumper with midships pump shows the developing style of post-war American fire engines.*

■ BELOW *This open cab-style fire engine is a 1958 Mack pumper.*

Merryweather turntable ladders were also used. The auxiliary fire crews used a number of extra fire boats to supplement the maritime and dockland firefighting resources of the professional crews. The German fire service tended to rely on its existing vehicles, which included Mercedes and Opel pumping engines, and Magirus and Metz turntable ladders.

The 1950s saw a wider use of diesel engines, and by 1960 the first automatic gearbox systems for fire engines were in use in Europe. The increasing use of alloys and plastics in bodywork design greatly increased the store of firefighting and rescue equipment that fire engines could carry. Power steering and braking systems were also becoming standard, as were robust safety cabs to protect the crew in the event of a traffic accident.

TYPES OF FIRE ENGINE

While modern fire engines may vary in their outward styling and design, they can be grouped in three general types – those that pump water, high rise rigs and specialist vehicles. High rise rigs have extending ladders

or booms that may reach up to 40m/130ft. These may be turntable and tower ladders or aerial ladder platforms with fitted cages on the uppermost sections. The operational roles of the range of specialist vehicles included providing crews and equipment for rescue, breathing apparatus, foam units, protection against chemical and hazardous material, salvage, ventilation, lighting, command and crew refreshment functions.

Fire engines that pump water are known variously as pumps, pumpers or water tenders. Their primary function is to provide a firefighting water attack, and they are generally regarded as the fire service's workhorses. Every city and rural fire brigade is likely to have at least one pump, and it is this type of fire engine that will almost certainly attend every emergency fire call-out.

Pumping fire engines incorporate a water tank that feeds the fire pump to provide a

■ BELOW *A 1972 PACO/Grumman heavy pumper.*

firefighting stream as soon as the appliance arrives at a fire, and before an alternative source of water is located. These first firefighting water jets are fed through hose tubing coiled on a revolving reel, often one on each side of the fire engine, or through hose

■ OPPOSITE *A 2002 Ferrara/Spartan 6x4 mid-mount aerial ladder shows the lines of a modern-day American fire engine.*

It can either produce a water jet that will directly knock down flames or a finely atomized spray to protect the crew from intense radiated heat. Pumps also carry a range of ladders, breathing sets, lighting and rescue equipment including cutting and lifting gear. In some rural areas, pumps have evolved into general-purpose fire engines that carry certain firefighting and rescue equipment that would normally be distributed over several fire engines in an inner city situation.

A wide range of chassis, engine power and transmission units can be found in fire engines across the world today, and most manufacturers provide a vehicle tailored to a fire brigade's precise needs. Many modern rural fire pumps are all-wheel drive with a high-ground clearance to allow for off-road operations, while a number of manufacturers have produced

lines of various sizes, either flaked (folded in lengths) ready for instant use or rolled-up in the fire engine lockers. Pumps usually carry about 0.8 kilometres/½ mile of hose, and shortly after getting to work at a fire one of the crew will connect the pump to a nearby street water main to maintain a supply of water.

■ ABOVE *A 1989 Ford/S&S 6x4 tanker with midships mounted pump.*

FIREFIGHTING INNOVATIONS

On a modern fire engine, the pump is capable of providing water at high pressure through hose lines fitted with an adjustable nozzle.

■ BELOW *A midships mounted Hush pumper of Fredericksburg Fire Department, USA.*

narrow-bodied compact fire engines to cope with narrow twisting roads. Many fire engines built for use in hot climates have air-conditioned crew cabs. In some cases the manufacturer designs and builds the complete vehicle, while others construct the bodywork and various fire pump engineering installations and mount it on a suitable commercial chassis/cab of a fire brigade's choice.

Modern fire engines have plenty of shiny metal and colourful bodywork. Red, orange and white colour schemes are commonplace, often enhanced by fluorescent stripes or panels to maximize the fire engine's conspicuousness, both en route to and while working at an emergency incident. A particular feature of modern fire engines is their warning devices. Electronic directional wailers, sirens, hooters, and powerful blue and red rotating flashing beacons are there to warn other road users of a fire engine's approach, often at high speed. Importantly for anyone trapped in smoke or under debris, the sound of an approaching fire engine is reassurance that rescue is imminent.

■ RIGHT *This Carmichael-bodied Volvo fire rescue unit is one of six such vehicles introduced in 1991 by London Fire Brigade.*

■ BELOW *This Magirus-bodied Iveco 4x4 light pump is run by Kellinghusen Fire Brigade in Germany.*

EARLY LADDERS

Although the use of single-section ladders can be traced back to the Roman *vigiles*, the real development in firefighting ladders came about during the early part of the nineteenth century, when multi-section ladders made it possible for firemen to reach upper floors.

MOBILE FIRE ESCAPES

In the early nineteenth century, London had a number of permanently manned 'street escape' stations sited on certain strategic street corners across the capital for rescuing people trapped in burning buildings. The first street corner stations were funded by voluntary contributions and were independent of London's fire brigade, but in 1866 the Metropolitan Fire Brigade took full responsibility for them.

Each station consisted of a cabin to house the watchman and a 15m/50ft wheeled wooden ladder made up of three extending sections that could reach the third floor windows of buildings. When a fire occurred, the ladder would be quickly pushed to the scene then

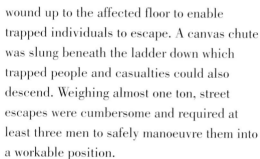

■ ABOVE *Compressed air was used to extend this early German 18m/60ft ladder.*

■ BELOW *Firemen in 1910 Vienna use hook ladders to take a line of hose up to the upper floors of a building. The coiled hose drum has been detached from the nearby fire engine.*

wound up to the affected floor to enable trapped individuals to escape. A canvas chute was slung beneath the ladder down which trapped people and casualties could also descend. Weighing almost one ton, street escapes were cumbersome and required at least three men to safely manoeuvre them into a workable position.

Before long the escape ladders, together with their large carriage wheels, were mounted on specially designed horse-drawn fire engines. These mounted escape ladders had a quick release mechanism and were normally manned by four firemen and a coachman. The teams were able to respond to an alarm and effect rescues very quickly, and were closely followed by the horse-drawn pumps, which tackled the fire itself. Due to their speedy and effective response to fire calls, the horse-drawn escape ladder soon became a permanent part of the London brigade's first line response, leaving the city's street corner ladder fire stations to be gradually phased out.

In America the development of high-rise buildings led to the design of even longer mobile fire ladders for both rescue and firefighting access purposes. By the late 1890s the larger city fire departments were using

■ RIGHT *An 18.2m/60ft hand-operated turntable ladder c.1910. Hand winding provided the power for the various movements of the ladder.*

■ BELOW RIGHT *A 1921 Morris Magirus 22.8m/75ft turntable ladder. The ladder sections were powered by electric motors.*

hook and ladder trucks – horse-drawn fire engines with a main ladder comprised of several wooden sections mounted on a long two-axle wagon. At the scene of a high-rise fire such a ladder would be manually wound up to its maximum working height of 20m/65ft. Once extended, the entire ladder could be rotated through 360 degrees. Hook and ladder trucks also carried a number of smaller ladders for low-level use and long pole-mounted hooks. The latter were for pulling down ceilings and partitions to ventilate premises during firefighting operations, and to ensure that fires were properly extinguished and no smouldering remnants were overlooked.

As American buildings increased in height in the early twentieth century, hook and ladder trucks were eventually replaced by longer aerial ladders, especially when early motor vehicles became available for fire department use.

■ LEFT *A London Fire Brigade officer uses a megaphone to shout instructions to a fireman on a horse-drawn hand-operated 23m/75ft turntable ladder during a 1905 drill session.*

■ BELOW *A Paris Fire Brigade c.1920 hand-operated 18m/60ft wheeled escape ladder is mounted on a Delahaye chassis. At the fire it would be released from the chassis before being put to work.*

Aerial ladders were able to reach up to 26m/85ft. The longest vehicles were fitted with a rear steering axle and needed a steersman at the back to negotiate tight turns en route to a call-out.

In Europe the arrival of the petrol engine heralded a new generation of high-rise fire service ladders of metal construction. Combined with new manufacturing and engineering techniques, including the use of gas and hydraulic power, these new ladder fire engines were soon to revolutionize aerial firefighting and rescue operations.

THE DEVELOPMENT OF LADDERS AND PLATFORMS

Wheeled wooden escape ladders, which were well established in Great Britain by the late nineteenth century, were the precursors of modern extending ladders. Usually constructed of three sections, they could be wound up to about 15m/50ft to allow people trapped by smoke in buildings above a fire to climb down to safety. They also allowed firemen some access into a burning building at upper levels, although it was not until the availability of the first self-contained breathing sets in the twentieth century that extensive firefighting inside buildings was possible.

In America, where the equivalent to the wheeled escape ladder was the hook and ladder truck, fire brigades started to look for better and longer mobile rescue ladders. In 1888, the E. B. Preston Company of Chicago, Illinois, constructed the first all-metal aerial ladder, although this still had to be extended

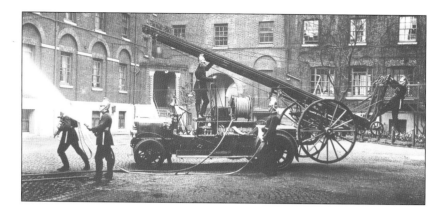

manually. The longer versions of these aerial ladder trucks were articulated and often needed a rear tillerman to steer the vehicle's back wheels round city street corners.

In Europe aerial ladder development was not far behind. In 1892 the German company Magirus constructed the first turntable ladder, where the extending section was mounted on a rotating turret able to turn through 360 degrees at various angles of depression. As with the first US aerial equivalent, this Magirus turntable ladder was built on a horse-drawn trailer and was extended manually. By the turn of the century, however, Magirus had perfected a powered elevation system using carbon dioxide gas. Other movements still relied upon hand-winding gear and the physical strength of firemen to winch the ladder sections up to the required working height.

■ TOP *During a 1910 London Fire Brigade training session, the 15m/50ft wheeled escape ladder is about to be slipped off the Merryweather vehicle, and manually wound up to its working height.*

■ ABOVE *Originally horse drawn, this American-built c.1920 26m/85ft rear-steer ladder of Lynn Fire Department, Massachusetts, has been converted to motor traction using a Knox Martin tractor.*

■ FAR LEFT *A 1914 23m/75ft Merryweather turntable ladder is put through its paces.*

Daimler, another German manufacturer, produced several early turntable ladders, some of which were mounted on a battery-powered electric chassis. In 1906, Magirus introduced the first truly motorized petrol engine-driven turntable ladder vehicle, although it relied on hand-winding for its extension and other movements. Two years later, Merryweather constructed the first British 23m/75ft turntable ladder, the various movements of which were entirely powered by a gearbox driven directly by the vehicle's petrol engine. The combined achievements of Magirus and Merryweather meant that all the movements of the aerial ladder – extension, elevation and training through 360 degrees – could now be driven by a cable-and-gear mechanism. American aerial

■ LEFT *In 1937 London Fire Brigade took delivery of a number of 30m/100ft all-steel Leyland/Metz turntable ladders. Here, a fireman surveys the London rooftops from the top of one of these new aerial fire engines.*

■ ABOVE RIGHT *This 1938 Leyland/Metz 30m/100ft turntable ladder served with the Lancashire County Fire Brigade, UK, until 1961. The rear nearside operating controls and gauges are clearly visible, together with the water pump mounted beneath the driving position.*

ladder makers soon followed suit, especially Pirsch who already was a pioneer in the development of all-metal ladders.

Another early twentieth-century development was the use of high-rise ladders as water towers for projecting a powerful jet into the upper floors of tall buildings. Increasingly, ladders had a hose line with a nozzle fitted to the uppermost extension and were able to reach 30m/100ft when extended.

Through the 1930s and 1940s the working heights of ladder fire engines continued to increase. In 1933 Merryweather delivered a

■ LEFT *A London Fire Brigade 1921 Morris Magirus 23m/75ft turntable ladder responds to a fire call.*

■ RIGHT *An American hand-operated water tower in action at a major tenement fire c.1930.*

30m/100ft turntable ladder vehicle to Hong Kong. Leyland/Metz supplied a 45m/150ft five-section turntable ladder to Hull Fire Brigade in the UK in 1936. In 1942, American LaFrance built a 38m/125ft aerial ladder for the Boston Fire Department.

By the 1930s the newer American aerials and water towers were using hydraulic power. In 1930 American LaFrance built a 20m/65ft water tower for New York that could deliver 38,590 litres/8,500 gallons per minute through multiple nozzles. One year later Pirsch produced the first fully hydraulic-powered aerial ladder truck. In Europe the primary manufacturers of turntable ladders continued to be the German companies Magirus and Metz, along with the British manufacturer Merryweather, based in London.

HYDRAULICS AND TURNTABLES

Hydraulic power did not completely replace mechanical ladder drives on turntable ladders in Europe and elsewhere until the 1950s, however. By then the hydraulic platforms, a natural development of the turntable ladder concept, had made an appearance. These aerial fire engines consisted of several articulated booms with a fitted cage at the head, all mounted on a rotating turntable. For the first time a firefighter working in the cage

■ ABOVE LEFT *A Japanese 30m/100ft turntable ladder of Sunagawa Fire Brigade.*

■ ABOVE CENTRE *Osaka Fire Brigade crew work the cage of a modern aerial ladder.*

■ ABOVE RIGHT *During the early stages of a fire in residential flats, the operator of this aerial ladder platform edges the cage nearer to the smoke-filled building.*

■ LEFT *A 1989 Seagrave 30m/100ft ladder of the Yonkers Fire Department, New York, sets to work at a routine incident.*

at the top of a hydraulic platform had complete control over the fire engine's movements. A prominent manufacturer of hydraulic platforms was the British firm Simon Engineering, whose Snorkel brand name became synonymous with hydraulic platforms in many countries.

In the latter half of the twentieth century the design and functional style of turntable ladders and hydraulic platforms began to be merged. The Finnish company Bronto pioneered telescopic booms that carried a parallel-trussed steel ladder alongside. Some modern larger aerial ladder platform trucks have a height capability of up to 40m/130ft. Such large aerial fire engines require the weight stability of a four-axle chassis and have rigid jacks on each corner of the chassis base to help to counteract the forces at play when the heavy steel ladder or platform sections are extended. The cages of these vehicles are able to accommodate up to eight rescued people and are fitted with full operator controls. They also have connections

■ ABOVE LEFT *This American 1918 Mack ladder truck shows the long wheel base of this type of fire engine.*

■ ABOVE RIGHT *A Volvo/Bronto aerial ladder platform soars above a major office block fire, enabling the crew to direct a powerful jet down on to the flames.*

■ LEFT *A number of Austin K4 18m/60ft hand-operated Merryweather turntable ladders were provided by the British government during World War II to supplement the fire engines of civilian fire brigades.*

for an air supply for breathing sets and are fitted with floodlighting. Other important features are water drencher sprays around and underneath the cage to provide a water curtain that protects the cage operator and occupants from convectional and radiated heat.

The speed of deployment of an aerial ladder or platform is always critical, and considerable training is required for its operation. The control systems are very sophisticated, with the latest models utilizing computer and advanced engineering technology. When an operator gets to work, the vertical stability of the ladder is paramount. All movements of the ladder, often with the upper sections operating at great height, are governed by safety and stability factors, which must take account of the condition and horizontal level of the road surface as well as weather conditions.

SPECIALIZED FIRE ENGINES

Until the beginning of the twentieth century most fire engine development was concerned with pumps, which were moved to the scene of a fire and operated successively by hand, horse power, steam and then finally petrol and diesel, in order to provide a continuous and plentiful supply of firefighting water. The diversity of today's specialist appliances clearly underlines the wide range of technical and logistical support that modern firefighters need for complex modern situations.

Until 1900 virtually all fires were still being put out using water streams, but by the early part of the twentieth century, manufacturing processes had been developed which produced outbreaks of fire that could not be tackled using water alone. The increasing use of the motor car, for instance, led directly to the expansion of the petrochemical industry and fuel storage sites and therefore higher risk of fire involving burning liquids such as petrol, fuel oil and other refinery by-products. As water simply runs off such burning liquids, often actually spreading the fire to unaffected

adjacent areas, other means of extinguishing fire had to be developed. After several attempts, particularly in the United States, a successful means of smothering petrol and oil fires was achieved using foam produced from bicarbonate of soda and other additives.

As soon as a successful foam concentrate was commercially available to fire brigades, special fire engines were commissioned to carry large quantities to tackle fires in fuel storage sites, refineries and the like. The London Fire Brigade introduced a foam tender,

■ ABOVE *The role of the Paris Fire Brigade lighting unit, seen here at work in c.1910, was to illuminate the firefighting scene during night-time incidents.*

■ LEFT *The London Fire Brigade's 1929 Dennis emergency tender carried a range of rescue tools that included breathing sets, cutting and lifting gear and resuscitation and lighting equipment. This fire engine had a recently introduced enclosed body.*

■ ABOVE *4x4 all-terrain vehicles are used as first strike and mobile control units during rural firefighting.*

ABOVE RIGHT *The rear end of this modern American pumper is packed with trays of flaked, or folded, hose ready for instant action.*

■ BELOW *Water tankers such as this American 4x4 example are vital in supplying water during firefighting operations in remote country areas.*

one of the world's first dedicated, or 'special', fire engines, in 1910. Mounted on a Leyland chassis, it carried a tank that could take 2,273 litres/500 gallons of foam compound and plenty of hose and special nozzles. As soon as it was fed with a water supply from a pumping fire engine, the foam tender could mount a concentrated attack.

Increasing mechanization and the growth of transport systems led to new types of accident from which victims occasionally had to be extricated using specialized equipment. As a direct result of these increasing non-fire emergency calls, fire brigades began to ask fire engine manufacturers to customize vehicles so they could carry all the equipment they needed for fighting particular types of fire and other emergencies.

Again, the London Fire Brigade was in the forefront of these new developments. In 1919 it introduced two emergency tenders, both on a Dennis chassis, equipped to deal solely with non-fire accidents and emergencies. The appliances carried lighting sets driven by a portable petrol-engine generator, lifting jacks, flame-cutting gear and a range of hand-operated cutting tools. Previously firefighting breathing sets had been fairly primitive, with a diving-style air supply line fed by bellows operated outside the building on fire. The emergency tenders carried innovative one-hour duration oxygen breathing sets and spare cylinders for use at deep-seated serious fires.

Fire service special vehicle applications soon grew to include hose-laying trucks. These were a radical development, even though many brigades had for some years provided manually drawn hose carts and, later, motor vans to convey additional rolled hose supplies to a fire. These hose-laying vehicles were designed to lay hose from the back of the van on the move at 30 kmh/19 mph. Sometimes up to 1.6km/1 mile long, the large-diameter hose relayed water from large trunk mains to the scene of a major outbreak.

By the 1950s most urban brigades ran one or more mobile command and control units, which were often based on a coach-type chassis. The unit would attend larger and more serious fires where strategic control and deployment of firefighters and resources was critical to the

■ LEFT *A mobile command unit, based on a Volvo coach chassis, provides a critical role at major incidents.*

success of the operation. Based at the unit, the fire commander would direct operations and receive reports on the progress of the firefighting effort. All reinforcements, radio communications, liaison with police, paramedics, traffic, and utility services would also be co-ordinated from the unit, as well as refreshments, relief crews and press contact.

Other modern day 'specials' include water tankers, or bowsers, for carrying large volumes of water to areas, usually rural, where existing water supplies are scarce. The largest of these water tankers are articulated, multi-axle vehicles capable of carrying up to 36,000 litres/7,920 gallons of water in one load.

Salvage tenders are usually mobilized to certain major or protracted fires to provide a concentrated effort to mitigate water and smoke damage to artefacts and business stock. They can also assist in the extraction of smoke from the affected premises using high-powered fans.

Lighting units provide crucial illumination across firefighting and rescue arenas, known in fire brigade parlance as the 'fire ground'. This can also include lighting the inside of fire-damaged buildings. Lighting units have a large electrical generating capacity, both on the fire engine and portables. They are also equipped with telescopic halogen lighting masts and a range of other lighting equipment.

Usually designed as a travelling self-contained kitchen, canteen vans provide meals for up to several hundred firefighters at a time. Dehydration, especially in hot weather, is a recognized hazard of firefighting, and these kitchen stations fulfil an important function.

DEMOUNTABLE EQUIPMENT MODULES
Modern special appliances are increasingly based on self-contained demountable

■ BELOW *During the 1970s, demountable equipment pods gained popularity with fire brigades around the world. This breathing apparatus major incident unit demountable pod is put into place whenever many breathing sets are in use at an incident. It can provide the constant servicing and air cylinder replacement that will be required.*

■ LEFT *This airport foam tender shows the centre-mounted nozzle used to extinguish flames in the fire engine's path.*

■ BELOW *This light rescue tender carries a range of tools and equipment used at non-fire emergencies.*

equipment modules, so that functional units can be rapidly assigned to a prime mover for speedy transport to an emergency. At the scene the demountable unit can be dropped off to release the prime mover for other duties.

'Demountables' have grown to include the following specialist areas: chemical and hazardous material units (providing special protective suits, breathing sets, leakage containment equipment, decontamination facilities etc); breathing apparatus units (full servicing facilities for the breathing sets in use at a major incident); and heavy rescue units (very powerful heavy-duty specialized lifting, spreading and cutting equipment needed for rail and aircraft accidents).

■ LEFT *A remote-controlled tracked vehicle used for forcible entry.*

■ BELOW *A heavy rescue tender carries a greater range of more powerful tools and general rescue equipment.*

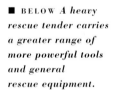

AIRBORNE FIRE ENGINES

The first flying fire engine was developed in America as early as 1918, when the San Diego Fire Department commissioned a Curtiss aircraft to provide a rapid firefighting response to outlying districts of its area. The aircraft was powered by a 110hp 6-cylinder engine and could reach a speed of 112 kilometres/70 miles per hour. Carrying a crew of two firemen, its firefighting equipment consisted of two 3-gallon water extinguishers, and four carbon tetrachloride chemical extinguishers.

While the success or otherwise of this pioneering effort is not readily recorded, it does illustrate that innovative fire chiefs were not slow in utilizing new and radical methods to speed up response time to outbreaks of fire. It was not until after World War II, however, that the use of aircraft for firefighting really came into its own, when development work by several Canadian fire departments led to the first use of 'water bombing' techniques from adapted aircraft to combat forest and grassland fires.

Before long the technique, which involves repeatedly dropping large quantities of water on to a country fire area, was commonplace, particularly in North America and Australia where forest and scrub fires often devastated vast areas. Modern firefighting aircraft are able to deliver up to 27,300 litres/6,000 gallons of water in a single drop. Fire-retardant chemicals are often added to the water to increase the effectiveness of each bombing run.

Helicopters fitted with large under-slung plastic and canvas buckets are also used during the forest-fire season. Although the water payload of a helicopter does not match that of a large fixed-wing aircraft, it has the advantage of being able to make repeated and effective water drops. It can quickly refill its

■ OPPOSITE *Canadair CL-215T turboprop amphibians are widely used as airborne fire engines. They are capable of dropping over 5,000 litres/1,100 gallons of water or foam mixture on to a fire.*

■ RIGHT *The moment of release as the Canadair drops a deluge of water.*

■ BELOW RIGHT *A Canadair CL-215T turboprop amphibian takes part in trials on a burning building in Quebec, in July 1992.*

bucket by flying low with its scoop over a river, lake or pond that may lie close to the scene of the fire. Alternatively, a helicopter is able to hover above firefighters while they refill the reservoir using fire hoses.

Several fire departments, including that of Tokyo, have the dedicated operational use of their own helicopters and these can be invaluable for rapidly transporting firemen to tall buildings and rescuing people from them. Brigades that do not have the financial resources to purchase or lease their own helicopter usually have arrangements whereby the nearest civil or military helicopters can be made available at very short notice.

Helicopters are also invaluable for transporting equipment and fire crews to an emergency, such as a serious fire or a rail or road crash, that is not easily accessible. Modern twin-engine helicopters can carry up to nine firefighters or a payload of around 1000kg/ 2200lb. Using radio and thermal imaging links, a helicopter hovering above a major incident or large-scale forest or grassland fire that threatens to spread out of control can provide valuable aerial reconnaissance.

FIREBOATS

Modern fireboats are floating fire engines. Ship fires are often protracted affairs, so fireboats are designed to operate as self-contained maritime firefighting units. In addition to being able to produce a barrage of firefighting water jets through a powerful pumping capacity, modern fireboats are equipped with breathing apparatus servicing facilities, including air compressors for recharging cylinders.

Fireboats were first developed during the early nineteenth century to combat a number of serious ship fires and dockland area conflagrations. As manually pumped land fire engines were slowly developed and improved, several engineers saw the potential of mounting a fire pump on board a boat, with the fire pump suction hose dropped over the side to tap the unlimited water supplies all around. In 1840 the London-based fire engine manufacturer Merryweather supplied an 18m/60ft iron-hulled fireboat to St Petersburg. The on-board manual pump required 50 men to get it to optimum performance.

When steam power began to be widely used to power land fire engines, it was also applied to fireboat design. By 1860 the London Fire Engine Establishment had installed a number of steam pumps on board special floating platforms based at strategic points on the River Thames and within London's huge and complex dockland area. These platforms were towed to a fire by a steam tug, and were known as a 'fire float'. By the 1870s both Boston and New York harbours had their own steam fire floats.

The first self-propelled fireboat, the *Beta*, was commissioned by London in 1898 and stationed at one of the capital's four floating fire stations on the River Thames. *Beta*'s steam boiler and steam plant provided both propulsion and firefighting water. With a draught of only 48cm/19in, the new London

■ ABOVE *A fire at the Thameside warehouse at Albany Mill near Blackfriars Bridge, London, 1791. The firefighting attack is being mounted from manual fire engines on board river boats.*

■ BELOW LEFT *This typical purpose-built firefighting tug has an inbuilt hydraulic platform to reach the upper deck of vessels.*

■ BELOW *The London Fire Brigade fireboat, Beaver, seen here in about 1910, towed a fire float (right) that carried the steam-driven pumps for the water jets.*

■ TOP LEFT **Firefighter**
protects the Boston
waterfront.

■ MIDDLE LEFT *New*
York Harbour has
several fireboats.

■ BOTTOM LEFT
Rotterdam Port
Authority has a total of
four patrol/fireboats.

■ ABOVE **Massed**
fireboats attack a fire
on a North Sea oil rig.

■ BELOW LEFT *A*
London Fire Brigade
fireboat lies off the
Palace of Westminster.

■ BELOW RIGHT *Two*
new London Fire
Brigade fireboats patrol
near the Millennium
Dome in 1999.

fireboat could come alongside warehouses at very low states of tide as well as get close in to burning vessels.

Fireboat development continued apace into the twentieth century. In 1925, the Los Angeles fire department's newest vessel could pump up to 61,000 litres/13,500 gallons of water per minute from no fewer than 13 separate deck-mounted nozzles. Since World War II the steady development of ever-larger ships carrying huge tonnages, ranging from container cargo to petrochemical products, has ensured that the availability of fireboats capable of dealing with any maritime fire outbreak continues to be critical. Some of the most up-to-date fireboats can be found in the frenetically busy port of Hong Kong, where hundreds of huge container ships dock daily. The Hong Kong fire department provides a permanent presence of up to four powerful multi-decked craft that are manned around the clock and ready to respond to maritime fires the moment they break out. Ports in the United States also have fireboat cover, while oil terminals throughout the world provide some fireboat cover to ensure that any outbreak of fire while an oil tanker is discharging its flammable load is dealt with immediately.

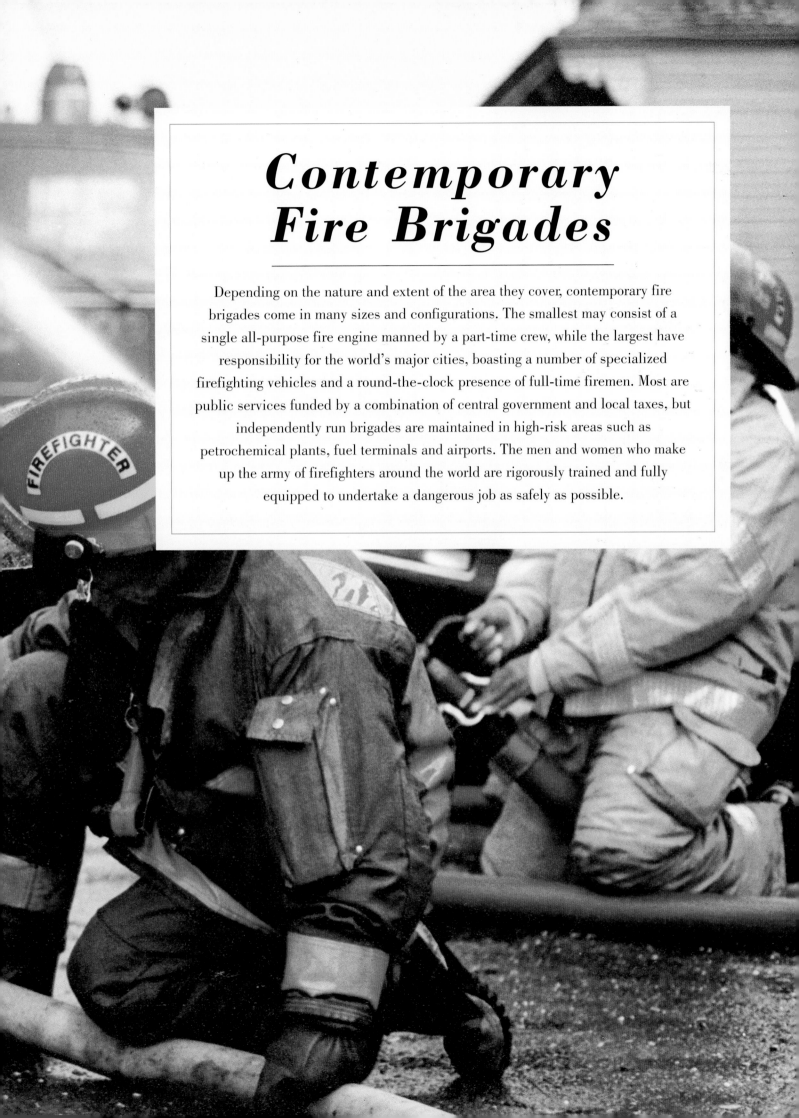

Contemporary Fire Brigades

Depending on the nature and extent of the area they cover, contemporary fire brigades come in many sizes and configurations. The smallest may consist of a single all-purpose fire engine manned by a part-time crew, while the largest have responsibility for the world's major cities, boasting a number of specialized firefighting vehicles and a round-the-clock presence of full-time firemen. Most are public services funded by a combination of central government and local taxes, but independently run brigades are maintained in high-risk areas such as petrochemical plants, fuel terminals and airports. The men and women who make up the army of firefighters around the world are rigorously trained and fully equipped to undertake a dangerous job as safely as possible.

FIREFIGHTING AND RESCUE EQUIPMENT

Modern fire engines carry a host of firefighting and rescue equipment, most of which would probably seem quite incomprehensible to nineteenth-century firemen, whose primary concern was to get a water stream on to a fire to restrict its spread to other buildings. In those days, they relied on lengths of leather hose joined together with screwed couplings and a nozzle (or branch in fire service parlance) at the end and a pump that, hopefully, would deliver a firefighting water jet. At worst the pump would be operated manually, but a progressive city brigade might own a powerful steam pump. The pump was on wheels and the hose was taken to fires on a handcart.

WATER PUMPS AND HOSE LINES

It was not until the twentieth century, with the arrival of the motor pump and particularly the first specialized appliances, that fire engines had enough space to stow other firefighting gear such as hose, portable pumps, hand tools and basic lighting. When the first all-enclosed fire engines were produced in 1929, bodywork styles allowed for even more stowage to accommodate the steadily growing range of

firefighting and rescue equipment. Modern fire engines need to carry a large amount of supplementary gear, so the ingenious design and use of locker space on a vehicle means that every available space can be utilized.

Water remains the predominant and universal extinguishing medium used by firefighters, with supplies usually available via a street hydrant or from a nearby natural source. Pumping fire engines carry varying quantities of water to enable an immediate firefighting attack on a fire for up to ten minutes, until an alternative source can be

■ ABOVE *From 1919 Dennis emergency tenders were used to provide pure oxygen breathing sets for deep penetration at serious fires. They also carried electric generators and floodlighting equipment.*

■ BELOW *Members of the Vienna Fire Brigade crew train with an early (c.1910) airline-fed smoke helmet and breathing set.*

■ RIGHT *Water has always been a firefighter's main weapon. Here, London Fire Brigade crews create a wall of water during a royal display in 1966.*

■ BELOW RIGHT *A Vienna Fire Brigade fireman tests an early twentieth-century back-packed compressed air breathing set.*

tapped. Depending upon the scale of the blaze, the on-board water will be pumped through either a small-diameter high-pressure hose reel or a larger-diameter hose line.

The on-board tank will have to be refilled by hose from a local water supply as soon as is practical. Fire engines that operate in rural areas also carry portable pumps, which can be carried to a river, lake or pond to pump water from that point. Another way of getting water to a fire is to run a shuttle, using the on-board tanks of several pumps, to ferry water to the fire scene. This is then transferred to the tank of the pumping engine operating there.

Hose lines, which are either rolled or stowed folded ready for quick deployment, come in a variety of diameters, and most pumping engines carry about 600m/2,000ft altogether. A range of hose connectors and adapters enable different combinations of hose to be used together to maximize water usage.

Other extinguishing equipment carried on pumping fire engines includes foam compound, which when mixed with water and aerated provides copious supplies of foam that may be needed to blanket the surface of burning liquids such as petrol or oil fuel. Smaller quantities of foam are provided from portable extinguishers carried on board. If a burning liquid fire involves very large quantities of flammable liquid, as might be found in a refinery or fuel storage depot, the use of a dedicated foam tender would be necessary. Such an appliance is capable of producing tens of thousands of litres of foam per minute. Dry powder and carbon dioxide extinguishers are also carried for use on fires involving electrical installations, which require smothering.

Pumping fire engines carry several ladders on the roof. Alloy ladders have replaced the

traditional wooden versions, being more robust and requiring less maintenance. Various types of ladder are in use, but all have extending sections with the longest ladders reaching up to about 13m/45ft. Shorter versions are available for scaling fences, walls and other obstacles, and some of these come as combination ladders that meet a number of variable purposes. Some fire engines are specialized ladder vehicles, with aerial or turntable ladders, or platforms.

SAFETY AND CUTTING EQUIPMENT

Breathing sets are usually mounted behind the seats in the back of the pumping engine's crew cab, where they can be donned en route to a fire scene. A breathing set provides clean air for up to 50 minutes in the thickest toxic smoke, although this time will be significantly

reduced if the firefighter is working hard and therefore consuming more air. At major fires, where large numbers of breathing sets will be in use, a mobile breathing set recharge-and-servicing unit will be set up to replace empty air cylinders. A safety control board is deployed whenever breathing sets are used at an incident. This monitors each firefighting team inside a smoke-filled building, how much air they have in their cylinders and the recorded time at which they should emerge.

Thermal imaging cameras allow fire crews to see through the thickest smoke to quickly locate casualties or the seat of a fire, and are now essential items of equipment.

■ LEFT *Two firefighters use powerful cutting tools to release a trapped driver. Road crashes present fire crews with difficult and challenging rescues.*

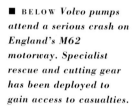

■ BELOW *Volvo pumps attend a serious crash on England's M62 motorway. Specialist rescue and cutting gear has been deployed to gain access to casualties.*

■ RIGHT *A fire crew works to free the trapped driver of a truck that has careered off the road and plummeted down an embankment in rural West Yorkshire, England. Access to such scenes can be challenging for firefighters and medical teams.*

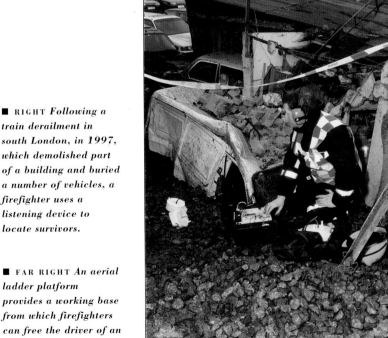

■ ABOVE *After a two-hour struggle, a fire crew successfully haul a bull out of a pit into which it had fallen. Animal rescues are often problematic because of location, the size of the beast and the fact that it is frightened.*

Rescue equipment for dealing with non-fire emergencies such as road crashes and industrial machinery accidents increasingly forms an important part of a fire engine's inventory. High-powered hydraulic cutting and spreading tools enable firemen to take the roof off a car in seconds, while sophisticated lifting and jacking equipment, including inflatable air bags, provides a range of tools to effect rescues from the most difficult and challenging situations. When an accident or crash is very serious, perhaps involving a train or a number of road vehicles, or in the event of a gas explosion that has demolished part of a building, an emergency or heavy rescue tender will attend to provide the additional cutting and lifting gear required. These dedicated fire vehicles are self-contained travelling workshops, often crewed by firefighters experienced in rescue work at major accidents.

■ RIGHT *Following a train derailment in south London, in 1997, which demolished part of a building and buried a number of vehicles, a firefighter uses a listening device to locate survivors.*

■ FAR RIGHT *An aerial ladder platform provides a working base from which firefighters can free the driver of an overturned lorry.*

Protective all-enclosing suits, usually two types, are carried to allow fire crews to safely work in an area deemed to be hazardous, such as at a fire or incident that involves a chemical substance, either at a plant or in transit. Chemical spill suits are worn over a regular firefighting uniform, together with gloves and a breathing set, to provide protection from the majority of chemical substances. Gas-tight suits provide a higher level of protection when dealing with certain highly hazardous materials that pose a serious threat if even a small amount comes into contact with skin or is ingested. A suit completely encloses a firefighter and his breathing set. Hazardous-material emergencies may also call for the use of a radiological measuring device.

■ ABOVE LEFT *A fire service line rescue team brings a casualty to safety after a pleasure park accident.*

■ ABOVE RIGHT *A Tokyo Fire Brigade robot rescue vehicle picks up a dummy casualty during a training exercise.*

■ BELOW *A fireman undergoes decontamination following an incident involving a hazardous and toxic material.*

SPECIALIZED RESCUE RESOURCES

In addition to a range of general purpose ropes and lines, a number of fire engines also carry line-rescue and abseiling gear, which is needed for rescuing people in precarious situations, such as halfway down a cliff face. Other specialist rescue gear includes mats for reaching people trapped in mud or quicksand, and even trailer-mounted inflatable boats. The rescue of pets and livestock may require specialist kit including slings and lifting apparatus such as sheerlegs and block and tackle.

Many firefighters are trained paramedics, and every fire engine carries a comprehensive first aid kit. A number also have defibrillation and resuscitation equipment, and the crew will be trained to deal with serious casualties with life-threatening injuries at the scene of an incident. Other on-board medical equipment can include specialist burn and wound dressings, a variety of splints, and neck and limb supports for people trapped in crash wreckage while extrication and rescue operations go ahead, sometimes before the arrival of a medical team.

Lighting at the scene of an emergency is also critical, and many modern fire engines have both built-in and portable generators capable of floodlighting a large area of operations. Some units have on-board telescopic masts to maximize lighting over a scene and portable clusters of lights to provide illumination at several points around an emergency site.

Other items of equipment likely to be found on fire engines are ventilation fans for drawing smoke out of an affected building, and various salvage items, such as waterproof sheets and dryers, to mitigate water damage caused by firefighting activities.

Communications are a vital part of firefighting and rescue operations. In addition to the personal radios that the crew deploy at the scene, the latest fire engines are equipped to act as a communication base, with a radio link to a control centre. There might also be a data link with a fast printer to provide the incident commander with vital hard copy information, for instance about the contents of a fire-affected building. Using further links into a dedicated chemical substance database, it is possible for the chemical properties of a particular hazardous material to be identified. Using the data link, the incident commander can receive precise instructions

■ ABOVE *Advanced carbon fibre air-cylinder technology has reduced the weight of modern breathing sets.*

■ BELOW LEFT *This Japanese fire service Mercedes-Benz Unimog was specially designed for use in earthquake conditions.*

■ BELOW RIGHT *A Kyoto Fire Brigade fireman, wearing a Japanese-designed protective uniform, gets a hose jet to work.*

on how to deal with the substance, as the wrong treatment could worsen the situation.

Every item of firefighting and rescue equipment carried on board a modern fire engine is subject to a rigorous regular inspection and testing regime. This ensures that every piece of kit will be in reliable and sound working order when firefighters need it – in a life or death situation seconds really do count. Regular inspection and testing also helps fire crews maintain practical knowledge of the workings of all their equipment, some of which may only be occasionally used.

FIREFIGHTING AND RESCUE OPERATIONS

When an emergency call comes into a fire station, the firefighters' objective is to get to the scene as quickly as possible, and in this the fire engine driver has a very critical task. Once in attendance at a fire, the driver operates the water pump and becomes responsible for supplying and maintaining both the immediate and long-term firefighting water needs of the crew.

The crew commander sizes up a fire situation within minutes of arrival, establishing first whether anyone is missing. The priority will be to locate and rescue anyone believed to be in an affected building. With the fire still spreading, a team in breathing sets will be ordered to penetrate and search the smoke-filled premises, taking a high-pressure hose line with them.

■ ABOVE *A massed rescue operation was put in place at Clapham Junction, South London, on the morning of 12 December 1988, following the collision of two commuter trains. Firefighters and medical teams extricated many passengers from the mangled wreckage; the crash left 35 dead and 46 seriously injured.*

■ LEFT *Firefighters of Detroit Fire Department get to work at a serious building fire.*

■ RIGHT *Tokyo Fire Brigade crews carry out the final stages of extinguishing a first floor fire above a shop. Several hose lines have been taken into the building off the ladders.*

All rooms are searched methodically by the crew as quickly as possible and, hopefully, casualties are found and rapidly removed to fresh air where they can be given paramedic aid, if necessary. If an aerial ladder vehicle is at the scene early on, it will be deployed to give the rescue teams fast access to upper floors, where people may be trapped by smoke rising from a ground-floor or lower-level fire.

As soon as all rescues have been carried out and a building is confirmed as being clear of casualties, the firefighting effort swings into top gear. If the fire is in the upper floors of a building, smaller ladders will be pitched to enable additional hose lines to work alongside the main aerial ladder in the task of locating and attacking the seat of the fire.

Modern firefighting tactics usually involve getting as close to the seat of a fire as possible before unleashing a powerful cooling water jet. This can be difficult in a hot smoke-filled home of two floors, but in a multi-floor commercial building with a complex layout, locating the seat of the fire is never easy.

■ BELOW LEFT *A fireboat crew help a distressed dolphin after it swam up the estuary of the River Thames.*

■ BELOW RIGHT *When the MV Sand Kite collided with the lock gates at the River Thames Barrier in 1997, the vessel's crew were safely taken off by a London fireboat.*

■ LEFT *A foam firefighting attack is launched on a 'crashed' light aircraft to prevent the ignition of spilt fuel during a training exercise.*

CONTROL AND SAFETY PROCEDURES

Quite often, the incident commander will have to dispatch more reserve crews with breathing sets into the building. In this case the control and safety procedures of those teams working inside wearing breathing sets are even more paramount. Even with the aid of thermal imaging cameras, which see through smoke, firefighters can face a protracted physical struggle to find the flames. While they are searching the building the fire could be spreading unseen through service ducts and shafts, and there is a danger that their escape route may be cut off.

As a fire burns on, it gets hotter and the smoke more dense. At some stage in operations, the incident commander may have to decide whether or not a forcible ventilation would be a practical option. Using special extraction fans, this would remove some of the heavy smoke conditions from inside the affected building. Unless a fire is completely extinguished, however, ventilation must be undertaken with great care, as in certain circumstances the action can increase the severity of the fire.

A fire has to be monitored right from the beginning of any firefighting operations in order to watch for signs of an impending 'flashover'. This much-feared phenomenon occurs when unburnt products of combustion suddenly ignite into a rolling ball of fire, often with explosive force. The changing colour, pressure and speed of smoke emission from the fire, and any weaknesses in the building

■ BELOW *Modern road crashes create increasingly difficult situations for fire and paramedic crews to deal with. In 1993 this runaway lorry crashed into a shopfront, killing six people.*

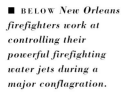

■ RIGHT *Thick smoke pours from a 16-storey office block in Kowloon in Hong Kong's worst fire tragedy for 100 years. The inferno broke out on 21 November 1996, killing 39 people and seriously injuring 90 others, and was attended by some 300 firefighters.*

■ BELOW *New Orleans firefighters work at controlling their powerful firefighting water jets during a major conflagration.*

structure are all indicators of a fire's behaviour, and at any point the incident commander may consider withdrawing all crews if their safety is under threat.

As a large-scale firefighting effort continues, reinforcing crews arrive continually and report to the control point that will be established at an early stage to co-ordinate the operation.

If the fire is a serious one, perhaps in large commercial premises with a complex multi-floor layout, the incident commander will have set up several firefighting command sectors. The commander of each sector will report regularly to the incident commander via their personal radio. Such contact is critical to enable the incident commander to continually assess and monitor aspects of the overall progress of the firefighting effort, such as

■ LEFT *Arsonists have set fire to a house in a residential area, leaving the fire service to bring the blaze under control and minimize danger to property and the public.*

making sure the risk of fire spreading into unaffected buildings is under control.

As the operation progresses, the incident commander also has to consider a variety of other factors. These could include any of the following: floodlighting an incident after dark, provision of water supplies, deployment of reinforcements, the communications network, overall safety supervision, salvage work to minimize and mitigate water damage; and liaison with police, medical services, local authorities and the press.

Arson is a growing problem for fire brigades in many parts of the world, so if there is any doubt about how a fire started, the likely cause may need to be forensically investigated once the fire has been brought under control. This work is done by a special fire investigation unit manned by experienced firefighters trained in forensic investigation. In conjunction with the police, they survey and photograph the post-fire scene, assess the pattern of burning and take samples of fire-damaged material to find out if any traces of accelerants are present.

NON-FIRE EMERGENCIES

As the number of non-fire emergencies tackled by firefighters has grown significantly in recent years, many brigades now rescue more people

from non-fire emergencies than from fires. Operations at a non-fire situation can be just as challenging as for a fire, and follow the same general procedures. The sheer variety of call-outs at any time of the day and night can be staggering, ranging from freeing people trapped in lifts to locating survivors buried under

■ BELOW *Erupting fireballs were a constant hazard to firefighting operations during this huge 1992 fire in a chemical factory and warehouse in Bradford, England. It was tackled by 200 firemen.*

■ RIGHT *Following devastating storms that caused widespread flooding, tangled hose lines carry tens of thousands of litres of flood water per minute away from an affected area. Freak weather conditions can impose considerable burdens on firefighters.*

yet carefully, often alongside a paramedic or medical team who will try to stabilize the casualty as the rescue work progresses. At a road crash where a driver and a number of passengers may be trapped and badly injured in a compacted car, roof, doors and floors may have to be cut away to gain access to the injured. A further potential hazard comes from air bags or seat belt pre-tensioners that have failed to activate in an accident. Air bags can suddenly explode and seat belts might suddenly snap tight.

rubble caused by bombs or earthquakes, or from rescuing a family from a smashed-up car to dealing with a large-scale hazardous chemical spill.

A fire crew may have to use specialized cutting equipment to extricate a trapped person from a dangerous situation, working speedily,

When dealing with toxic chemical leaks, firefighters must don special all-enclosing protection suits before they begin work. Once they have made the situation safe, each crew member needs to be decontaminated under portable water-spray showers set up at the scene, and provided with clean clothing.

■ RIGHT *Rescue teams have had to cut through twisted and crumpled metal to extricate the drivers and passengers of three cars involved in this horrendous road traffic accident on a British motorway. The disaster was caused by a long steel beam load breaking away and swinging across the adjacent carriageway.*

URBAN BRIGADES

The history of organized fire brigades shows that the biggest and sometimes most challenging fires have occurred in heavily populated city areas, where the threat to life and property is never far away. As most fires are caused by human activity, such areas have an inherently high fire risk, and where a population lives and works in very crowded and cramped conditions with little or no provision of fire precautions, the risk is even higher.

Tall buildings, crowded shopping and business centres, older-style properties with

■ BELOW LEFT *A turntable ladder helps combat a major fire at night in a city centre.*

■ BELOW RIGHT *Urban terrorism, such as this bomb attack on a city tower, causes large-scale destruction that calls on the full resources of modern firefighters.*

few fire precautions or means of escape, coupled with traffic congestion, narrow, over-parked streets and blocked access for fire engines make life even more difficult for city fire crews when time is of the essence. To make matters worse, city centres often have to cope with large daily influxes of commuters on trains and roads and seasonal population fluctuations caused by large numbers of tourists.

To cope with the ever-present threat of fire, brigades in large cities and towns provide round-the-clock professional crews ready to

■ RIGHT *The increasing incidence of arson, whether it involves torching a car or destroying a building, is a continual problem, especially for urban brigades.*

■ BELOW *Firemen outside a north London terraced dwelling give external support to colleagues working inside. These will be wearing breathing sets as they locate and extinguish the seat of the fire.*

turn out immediately after an alarm is raised. A three or four-hour shift system ensures that one group of the fire station's workforce is on duty at any time, day or night, with sufficient qualified firefighters to man all the station's fire engines. Shifts, or watches, can be up to nine hours during the day period and up to 15 hours at night.

In many countries, the response of the fire service to emergencies is governed by statutory regulations or codes of practice. These graduate the different areas served by each fire station into three or four fire risk categories, taking into account the potential fire threat to both life and property. In a city or large town, the highest categories are likely to be those buildings in streets and districts where the threat of fire is known to be considerable. Such premises might include high-rise and tenement flats with few alternative exit staircases, or industrial factories or workshops using processes that involve a significant risk of fire. When a fire call is received, the number of fire engines sent in response is directly linked to the known fire risk category, which also determines the precise time limits for the fire brigade's response.

In the highest fire risk category areas, a call-out to a fire in a high-rise tenement in the middle of the night will see at least three pumping engines, or pumps, responding along with at least one aerial ladder. In such a case, the first pumps are required to be at the scene within a few minutes of receipt of the original alarm call. Similarly, a fire call to a large urban factory known to have large quantities of flammable petrochemicals and other hazardous materials on site will, in addition to pumps, also bring the attendance of a foam tender and other specialist vehicles that might be needed.

Conversely, only two pumps will be despatched to a detached dwelling house. This system means that in a city or large town, the overall fire service response to a call-out can come from a number of different fire stations. The priority of the brigade command centre, which receives all emergency calls for the area and alerts the appropriate fire stations, is simply to get sufficient fire engines, crewed by sufficient firefighters, to an emergency scene to immediately deal with the potential situation, whatever it may be. Once pumps and other fire engines have been despatched, the command centre must also monitor the overall fire cover for the city area to ensure there are enough fire engine resources to get to the extremes of the area within the required time limits. If the first crew commander at the scene requires immediate reinforcements, either for firefighting or rescue purposes, these will be rapidly mobilized from the nearest fire stations with available crews and equipment.

All city fire stations will almost certainly have several pumping engines attached, and many will have a high-rise aerial ladder together with other specialist vehicles according to the various fire risks in the station area and surrounding community.

Allocated fire station areas in cities tend to be fairly small and in the most heavily populated cities can embrace just a few blocks

■ ABOVE *New York firefighters contain a fire that has broken out in the engine compartment of a parked car.*

of streets. Fire crews know their individual station areas very extensively. Acquiring widespread local knowledge of fire risks plus a general familiarization with much of the locality and what goes on within the fire station area 24 hours a day is key to a firefighter's success. This knowledge will include the layout of the road network, street names, the location of street firefighting water hydrants and the access points leading into the larger building complexes, including high-rise structures and multi-basement layouts. It will also embrace the various entrances and exits of transport and subway systems in the fire station area. A sound understanding of the general layout of major industrial factories and manufacturing plants together with their fire alarm panels, sprinkler control points and the availability of water supplies is also crucial.

Even with round-the-clock firefighting provision, a number of serious inner city fires with high loss of life occurred during the latter half of the twentieth century, illustrating the difficulties involved in fighting urban fires.

HIGH-RISE FIREFIGHTING PROBLEMS
One such tragedy occurred in São Paulo, Brazil, on 1 February 1974, when a small fire broke out in the newly built 25-storey Joelma office block. Soon flames and smoke were pouring out of its windows, and several hundred office workers trapped above the flames found the inadequate staircase completely impassable in the thick, choking smoke.

The São Paulo Fire Brigade mounted a valiant rescue effort, but because the fire had spread upwards so rapidly, they could not reach the people trapped by the blaze. Furthermore, the inferno was fuelled by the plastic lining and panelling of the building.

■ LEFT *This fire in a 12th-floor south London flat shows the dangers of convected smoke and upwards fire spread. High-rise fires require special firefighting techniques.*

■ BELOW *Fire rapidly engulfs an empty six-floor office block in east London despite the efforts of 100 firefighters at the scene.*

Kowloon district. Fire crews were first called when fire was reported on a lower floor during the early evening, when many office workers were still inside.

Precious time was lost getting firefighting teams into the building because access doors were locked, during which the small fire had spread upwards via service ducting and lift shafts. Smoke and heat soon started to affect the upper floors. To make matters worse, the building had no proper fire exits and only a couple of staircases. As the horror developed,

Because the firefighting effort could not easily be taken inside the building, external hose jets had to be used, but were largely ineffective.

Many of the workers trapped by the smoke and flames eventually managed to get on to the roof. Meanwhile, those ladders that could be used were brought into position; they virtually groaned under the sheer weight of the injured, shocked and distressed victims who were able to get on to them and be assisted down. A rescue attempt was even made by means of lines fired to the building from a harpoon gun. After two hours or so, the flames had died down sufficiently for helicopters to land on the roof and snatch 80 survivors to safety.

Sadly, when the fire crews finally forced their way into the office block to damp down the collapsed debris, they found more and more bodies on all floor levels. In all, 227 workers died in this awful tragedy; this death toll could most certainly have been reduced if properly designed structurally protected fire escape routes had been provided and other fire precaution measures had been in place.

Another major city centre fire occurred on 21 November 1996, when flames engulfed a 16-floor commercial building in Hong Kong's

more than 300 firefighters were called to the blaze. Every available aerial ladder and hydraulic platform was rushed into use to pluck frenzied office workers from the windows where they were trapped high above the street.

The heat and smoke inside the building were soon unbearable. Metal windows melted and false ceilings collapsed, making internal rescue efforts highly dangerous. Many workers jumped to their deaths before firefighters on ladders could reach them. Other firefighters battled up the stairs, damping down the flames with high-power water jets as they went. Out of these awesome conditions, the Hong Kong crews managed to lead many workers into safety.

■ RIGHT *Firefighters at work during the final stages of dealing with a serious fire.*

■ BELOW *Teams of firefighters working in the roof void of this office complex in the heart of the City of London are managing to bring the fire under control.*

Some 21 hours after the first alarm the fire was finally brought under control. By then 39 bodies had been recovered and 90 workers had been seriously injured. Many others had been rescued, but more than 35 people remained unaccounted for. One senior Hong Kong fireman, Liu Chi-hung, lost his life when he plunged down a lift shaft while attempting a dramatic rescue, and a number of other firefighters suffered minor injuries.

Due to the immense scale of the structural and contents damage, the cause of the fire remains unknown, although it was later discovered that the building had no sprinkler system or an adequate fire alarm.

FIRE CREW STRUCTURE WORLDWIDE

The structure of fire crews and the fire engines they man varies around the world. In the United States, city fire departments and fire stations, or 'firehouses' as they are known, are organized into specific 'companies' whose sole purpose is to man pumping trucks, aerial ladders or rescue fire engines. Elsewhere, fire engines attached to city fire stations are generally crewed by firefighters who have a wide mix of skills and

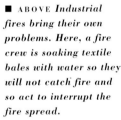

■ ABOVE *Industrial fires bring their own problems. Here, a fire crew is soaking textile bales with water so they will not catch fire and so act to interrupt the fire spread.*

qualifications across a range of disciplines. This can mean that the crew of a pumping fire engine for one tour of duty can man an aerial ladder the next. Each watch is under the command of an officer who is in charge of up to 30 or more firefighters, and each fire engine will have a crew commander, usually a junior.

In some countries, professional firefighters form part of a specific division of the military. French fire crews, known as Sapeurs-Pompiers, have been part of the army since Napoleonic days. Even though they operate as a self-contained fire brigade, they retain direct links with the armed services. Similarly, some firefighters in countries in Eastern Europe and the Middle East are also a uniformed part of the nation's civil defence organization.

Hong Kong has a very busy fire service whose risks vary from high-rise office and factory buildings, the densely populated

Chinese quarters in the waterfront districts, through to one of the world's largest ports. It also has the fire and rescue responsibility for Chek Lap Kok International Airport.

In addition to their firefighting duties, specialized groups in the uniformed personnel of fire services also carry out various fire prevention and safety duties in the world of commerce and industry, and the community at large. This work includes inspections of sprinkler systems, hose reels, fire extinguishers and alarm systems; checks on fire precautions in sleeping areas such as homes for the elderly, hotels and hostels; and general fire safety lectures to schools and other institutions. New building design also comes under fire service scrutiny at an early stage to ensure compliance with the relevant fire safety codes, including means of escape in case of fire, emergency lighting and smoke detection systems.

COUNTRY BRIGADES

Unlike their city and urban counterparts who have to employ full-time firefighters, rural and country fire brigades are generally staffed by retained firemen drawn from the local community. This cost-effective method of providing fire cover does have its limitations so can only be used where there is a relatively low risk factor, such as a low incidence of high-rise buildings and low concentrations of people. Fires and other emergencies do occasionally occur, but the presence of professional fire crews on permanent standby is just not financially practical.

Although rural fire departments are often funded directly by the community they serve, their fire engines and equipment are every bit as modern and sparkling as those found in inner city brigades. Rural and country fire stations are usually smaller than their urban counterparts but nonetheless house a number of fire engines, mostly of a pumping and rescue variety. These will inevitably be of a compact design style, often with 4x4 drive and a narrow overall body width for negotiating narrow country lanes.

One particular difference between city and rural brigades is that the area of a rural fire station is often very large and diverse. Outside the township or village will be an expanse of open country, and one of the principal risks will be farmland, bush, grassland and forest fires, which regularly occur during the dry summer months. Such rural firefighting is usually long, arduous and physically exhausting, demanding great resilience and reserves of stamina.

Retained firefighters need to live close to the fire station they serve and be available to respond to fire calls around the clock. This means having an understanding employer, as

■ OPPOSITE *The 1994 bush and forest fires in Crystal Peak, Nevada, involved several hundred firefighters.*

■ RIGHT *San Francisco Earthquake: The engine that put the fire out in the Mission district.*

■ BELOW *Sri Lankan villagers work together to beat out an undergrowth fire at the jungle's edge.*

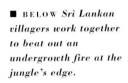

well as a sympathetic family. They are mobilized to fire and emergency calls by personal pager-style electronic devices that are carried at all times. In response to an alert the first fire engine will be on the road as soon as sufficient retained firefighters have arrived at the fire station to form a crew, usually of five or six. The turnout will be impressively quick and within minutes of the alarm being raised. In days gone by, rural crews would have been summoned by an electric siren, bell or even by a bugle or trumpet.

At the scene of most rural operations, firefighting water supplies are usually much less readily available than in a city or urban environment. Fire crews have to be adept at using any available natural water resource to be found in the vicinity – rivers, streams, lakes, ponds and sometimes swimming pools. Once located, this water is pumped through hoses to the scene of a fire, which may be a considerable distance away, using light portable pumps carried to the water source. The rigours and physical demands of rural firefighting can be likened to that of working amid a cross-country military commando course. On these occasions, personal radio contact links and co-ordination between crews is vital.

Laying out many lengths of hose to connect up to a remote water source is never a straightforward task and often is not practical

due to distance or difficult terrain. On such occasions many rural brigades operate a large water tanker to shuttle water from a remote source that is accessible from a road access point. The water tanker discharges its load,

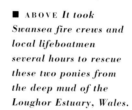

■ ABOVE *It took Swansea fire crews and local lifeboatmen several hours to rescue these two ponies from the deep mud of the Loughor Estuary, Wales.*

which can be up to 36,000 litres/8,000 gallons, into a temporary dam, or water tank, erected alongside the base pump. The pump draws its water from this supply to provide several constant firefighting jets while the tanker continues its ferrying operation. These water relays are not easy to regulate and call for plenty of physical effort and careful judgement to ensure that the water supply lasts.

The role of a firefighter in a rural area can be as demanding and dangerous as in an urban environment, because wild weather often strikes particularly hard. In many parts of the world, prolonged spells of dry weather bring the likelihood of fast-spreading grass, bush and forest fires, which threaten lives and property in the path of the rapidly advancing flames. A serious bush or forest fire requires a large-scale firefighting operation, often lasting for

■ LEFT *A fireman has no option but to manually pull a heavy hose line along the edge of a forest fire area as he works on the fire. Firefighting in this type of rural situation can be physically arduous.*

■ RIGHT *A difficult rescue operation is in progress to release the driver of this car, which has careered off the road and overturned. A medical team is also in attendance.*

■ RIGHT *Life is full of variety in a rural firefighting force. This fireman has been asked to rescue a hedgehog that had found its way up onto the roof of a country house in Lincolnshire, England.*

weeks. It will necessitate a huge logistical build-up to provide relief crews, feeding and refreshment facilities, water supplies and aerial support, both for reconnaissance and dropping water from the air (water bombing).

In recent years, parts of the United States and Australia have regularly suffered serious bush and forest fires, which have all caused loss of life, both human and animal, and immense destruction and disruption. In October 1991, for example, a huge bush fire in the Oakland district of California burned for many days and nights, destroying more than 3,000 separate buildings and eventually claiming 25 lives. Fire damage over an area of some 647 hectares/1,600 acres was conservatively estimated at more than $1.5 billion.

Three years later, a huge outbreak in New South Wales in Australia saw fire rapidly develop to engulf a woodland area of more than 9,700 hectares/24,000 acres. Four people were killed and more than 100 were injured. Twenty thousand firefighters were drafted in from

■ BELOW *A volunteer service fire truck from Marydel Volunteer Fire Service, Marydel, US.*

■ BELOW *Called out to deal with a simple hedgerow fire in Cornwall, England, a rural crew soon discovered that the fire was in fact large timber stacks burning out of control. With flames spreading in all directions, the crew had to quickly assess the situation, call for back-up and start containment.*

far afield to support the local teams, some professionals even arriving from distant city brigades. Eighty four helicopters and six planes were finally in use dropping water and fire-bombing various parts of the burning vegetation, working alongside more than 1,400 pumping engines and tankers.

Outbreaks of fire involving farms and farm machinery can also spread quickly, especially during the dry months of harvest time. Burning machinery, perhaps an overheated combine harvester or baler, can set fire to adjacent standing cereal crops, a fire which can run away at an alarming rate to provide a further challenge when the first pump arrives.

Agrochemicals, often stored and used on farms in some quantity, can readily present rural fire crews with difficult situations. Chemicals and hazardous substances can intensify a fire. Even if they are not directly involved in a fire, crews tackling this type of rural blaze will need to be ready to adopt a

high level of personal protection, using all-enclosing protective chemical suits together with breathing sets to safeguard them from exposure to or ingestion of toxic fumes. Once the chemicals have been dealt with in accordance with specialist advice, any of the crew who have had direct contact with the substances are likely to need full decontamination using portable water spray showers. Retained firefighters need to be particularly well trained and equipped to deal with this aspect of countryside operations.

Animal rescues are a common feature of rural non-fire emergency work. These literally come in all shapes and sizes when horses, cattle or sheep may get stuck fast in deep mud or bogged down in a slurry pit. The rescues can be difficult and of a protracted nature, often requiring plenty of equipment to be laid out before the rescue attempt begins. The weight of many farm animals will require the use of special animal slings, secured to cables and a powered winch mounted on a fire engine, or

■ BELOW *Using a special tripod and sling, rural firefighters struggle to release a steer stuck fast in mud.*

■ RIGHT *The crew of a Dennis/Simon hydraulic platform remove part of a fire-damaged roof.*

■ BELOW *As this aerial ladder goes into action, its operator's task will be complicated by overhead power cables.*

simply using a lifting block and tackle with ropes and lines via a sheerlegs tripod. The rescues usually have to be carried out under the supervision of a veterinary surgeon, as animals quickly become distressed and may need to be tranquillized before extrication and rescue is possible. Cleaning up after such incidents can be a pretty mucky and time-consuming affair, not just the various items of equipment but also the crews' uniforms.

Extremes of weather also provide for busy, sometimes chaotic, periods for rural fire brigades. The work can continue over a stretch of continuous day-and-night operations as the crews struggle to return a community back to normal. Storm force winds and rain can bring serious flooding, trapping people in their homes, and causing plenty of misery and suffering. Falling trees bring down power lines and often damage buildings. Vehicles can even be overturned and washed away.

Emergency call-outs occur at all times of the day and night throughout the year, and can

impact on the working, social and personal life of retained firefighters. Inevitably, the families of retained firefighters are drawn into the work of the fire service, and often support all the effort that goes into making a rural fire station work effectively. Quite often, there is a tradition of family firefighting service that goes back over a number of generations. Unsurprisingly, country townships take great pride in the achievements and service provided by their firefighters. It is not unusual to find that they are at the centre of the township community and its various activities, often being the focus and driving force of many fundraising and charity events throughout the year.

INDUSTRIAL SITUATIONS

During the considerable commercial expansion of industry and commerce in the nineteenth century, it became both common and sensible practice for companies with significant fire risks on their own premises to employ an in-house fire brigade. This ensured that in the

■ BELOW *Thick smoke turns day into night at this major fire in a chemical plant.*

event of an outbreak of fire an immediate firefighting response was on hand to extinguish or at least contain flames, which could threaten an entire factory or production plant, before the arrival of the public fire brigade.

WORKS FIRE BRIGADES

At first, works fire brigades were drawn from the company's ordinary workforce. In the event of a fire or other emergency, these men would quickly don their company fire uniforms and brass helmets then commence firefighting operations. The first works brigades relied on manual pumps, with the company name proudly emblazoned on the side. In larger factory and works complexes these were replaced by steam-powered pumps when they became available in the second half of the nineteenth century. Companies in the more profitable industries were quick to build proper fire stations within the factory complex, manned around the clock by a dedicated team of trained firemen.

One such early works fire brigade was that of the Hodges Gin Distillery in London's Lambeth district. Frederick Hodges, the distillery owner, took a personal interest in the whole business of firefighting, ensuring that his fire station was fully equipped and his firemen turned out in well-fitting smart uniforms and helmets that were also functional. He also built a 37m/120ft high observation tower so the firemen could keep a permanent watch for signs of fire outbreaks, both within the distillery and in the streets beyond.

Hodges' brigade became the first in London to replace their manual fire pumps with steam-powered pumps, taking delivery in 1862 of two Merryweather horse-drawn models, appropriately named Torrent and Deluge.

Hodges' new acquisitions could pump water jets 40m/130ft into the air at a rate of 636 litres/140 gallons per minute. His brigade's response to a call of "Fire!" was so fast that often they were the first to arrive at the scene, going on to play a significant firefighting role supporting the London Fire Engine Establishment's (LFEE) manual pumps at many large fires. At this time, the capital's public brigade, the LFEE, was vigorously resisting a move towards the introduction of steam-driven fire pumps. The effectiveness of Hodges's private fire brigade with its advanced equipment was undoubtedly one of the factors that led to the LFEE's eventual adoption of steam-powered pumps in 1863.

The development of works fire brigades continued unabated, and around 1905 some were beginning to introduce motorized fire engines every bit as grand and well equipped as those serving in the larger city brigades. By the early part of the twentieth century, many companies regarded on-site fire stations and dedicated firefighting crews as a positive step towards safeguarding their future prosperity, and the fire cover they gave was often more effective than that provided by the local municipal fire brigade. Many of the smaller

■ ABOVE *During a refinery fire training exercise in Cheshire, England, firefighters use one of the brigade's specialist ERF foam tenders to provide a powerful jet.*

■ BELOW *Working together as a team, a fire crew prepare to extinguish a leaking pipeline fire at a chemical plant in Cleveland, England.*

works brigades, however, were staffed on a casual basis by workers who could only be expected to provide an immediate 'first-aid' response until the municipal fire crews arrived. Nonetheless, there are many recorded instances of a works fire brigade successfully bringing a fire under control.

Over the past few decades, the comparative cost benefits offered by modern fire detection technology over the spiralling costs of keeping a dedicated fire team on site has led to a steady decline in the number of large commercial

companies prepared to maintain an in-house fire brigade. Today the fire defence of much of commerce and industry relies upon the proven effectiveness of intelligent smoke-detection and alarms allied to automatic fire-control methods such as sprinklers, water-sprays, and inert gas systems. Such technological improvements combined with greater emphasis on the fire-awareness-training of employees and in-house procedures has inevitably led to higher levels of commercial fire safety.

High-risk industries necessarily continue to run their own firefighting units to ensure an immediate on-site response to any emergency incident. On-site works fire brigades are specially trained in dealing with the particular dangers of fires and other emergencies caused by the industry products and materials. An outbreak of fire or a leakage, for instance, in any high-risk premises such as nuclear power installations, petrochemical refineries, chemical plants and large gas storage installations could rapidly pose a serious toxic, explosive or pollution threat to surrounding communities. On a different level, the potential for huge

■ ABOVE *A London Fire Brigade crew prepares to undergo decontamination by water spray after dealing with the leakage of a toxic chemical.*

■ RIGHT *A fireman in the cage of a Dennis/Simon hydraulic platform directs a powerful water jet into burning industrial premises.*

financial losses through stoppages following a fire at any of the large new production plants, such as in car manufacturing, or in a mega-sized warehousing complex, is unacceptably high for the businesses concerned.

Works fire brigades carry out general duties such as constant fire patrols. They are also responsible for the ongoing training of other employees in general fire safety awareness and precautions, including the proper action to be taken in case of a fire being discovered and practising the techniques of using fire extinguishers on live fire simulators.

The crews perform regular firefighting drills, and often exercise on site with firemen from the nearest municipal or county brigades. When responding to a fire in one of these special industrial situations it is critical that the public fire crews have a sound understanding of the general layout of the plant or complex and its firefighting facilities and systems. When the plant and public crews practise together, the teams often simulate real fire and emergency situations that involve the use of a whole range of firefighting procedures and equipment.

A LARGE SCALE INDUSTRIAL FIRE

In spite of all these precautions, industrial fires do get out of control, and one such occasion was 21 July 1992, a day that many firefighters, and others, in West Yorkshire will never forget. Early in the afternoon, the works fire team were called to a report of smoke in a raw materials warehouse at the Bradford plant of Allied Colloids, manufacturers of a wide range of specialized chemicals. The plant covered a site of approximately 16 hectares/ 40 acres and employed 1,600 people.

The fire team found that two cardboard drums of organic compound had begun to decompose, but decided that no further assistance was required. Some 50 minutes later, there was a sudden explosion in the same warehouse, and when the first pumps of the West Yorkshire Fire Brigade arrived within six minutes, a severe fire was already engulfing the building. Extra pumps were immediately requested.

As the first fire crews got to work, both firefighting and supervising the evacuation of workers, further flashovers and explosions occurred. Burning liquid chemicals soon became rivers of flame, spreading fire through the plant and into high stacks of drums storing various chemical products. Fireballs shot across the storage area, sending liquid fire up into the sky like a grotesque firework display. The black smoke blotted out the summer sunshine and cast an eerie darkness over the district around the burning plant.

More pumps were ordered to the scene, and soon 30 pumps, three aerials and ten support

■ ABOVE *This mill fire rapidly took hold on all floors and presented firefighters with a major task.*

tenders, with over 200 Yorkshire firefighters, were at work. A major problem was water. No fewer than 18 hydrants were in use at the height of the inferno, and a 1.6 kilometre/ 1 mile water relay was set up from a dam.

All residents downwind of the huge smoke plume were warned to keep their windows and doors shut. Later, the toxic chemical pollutants in the smoke led to fruit and vegetables being condemned, and for a while, even swimming in the local downwind rivers was banned.

The Allied Colloids fire was eventually brought under control by the early evening, after seven hours of intense firefighting efforts, often in the face of explosion and liquid fire. Fortunately no lives were lost, although 39 firefighters were injured and needed hospital treatment. The huge fire subsequently proved to be the largest blaze ever tackled by the brigade, and one that taxed the firefighting resources of the entire area.

AIRPORTS

From the earliest days of aviation, the risk of fire following a crash or spillage of fuel has been a major safety issue. However, it wasn't until the development of commercial aviation and the steady growth in the size of passenger-carrying aircraft that attention was focussed on the need for adequate aviation fire protection. This quickly became a priority as air travel distances increased across entire continents, necessitating the carriage of much greater fuel loads. From then on, airports had to train and maintain their own dedicated brigades to deal with all possible emergencies on their patch.

Several fire engine manufacturers had adapted existing water tender design for airfield firefighting early on, but real developments in aviation fire engines only began after World War II, when the Cardox Corporation in America designed a fire engine fitted with foam equipment that could blanket an aircraft fire. An integral foam compound tank linked to an in-built water tank produced an effective supply of firefighting foam that was then pressurized using carbon dioxide gas

■ LEFT *Exercises at the Fire Service College, in England, include techniques for quelling, containing and preventing aircraft fire.*

and discharged through a large rotating nozzle (also called a monitor) mounted on the roof of the fire engine.

Further developments followed and by the 1950s a range of airfield fire tenders became available, including some with all-wheel, cross-country rapid intervention capability. As the overall size and fuel capacity of passenger aircraft continued to grow so did the need for larger airport foam tenders that could carry

■ BELOW *Airfield foam and rescue tenders include a Simon Gloster Saro (foreground) and a Thornycroft Nubian model (background).*

■ RIGHT *An airport
fire rescue unit
equipped with a
rooftop-mounted
Snozzle. Mounted on
a telescopic boom, this
device is able to
penetrate an aircraft
fuselage and project
a powerful water
spray inside.*

■ RIGHT *US Air Force
firefighters clad in
close-proximity fire suits
and breathing sets
practise the rescue of a
trapped pilot during a
training exercise.*

■ BELOW *Norwegian
airport firefighters
train on a gas-fired
simulator that can
create a range of
aircraft fire scenarios.*

more foam compound and water together with a
wider range of powerful rescue tools. No sooner
had the first 6x6 airport fire tender made an
appearance, however, than the arrival of the
first commercial Boeing 747 Jumbo Jet
necessitated even bigger, faster and more
powerful airport fire and crash tenders.

By this time, diesel engines were replacing
petrol power in airport fire engines, and
automatic gearboxes were coming into use.

Other new features included a hydraulic platform facility to raise firefighters to the height of the tail-mounted engines of some new aircraft types. Typical of the new breed of airport crash tender was the Thorneycroft/Carmichael Nubian Major, a 6x6 vehicle powered by a 300bhp Cummins V8 diesel via semi-automatic gearbox that gave a speed of 64kmh/40mph in 41 seconds. The Nubian Major's 6,820 litre/1,500 gallon water capacity combined with a 700 litre/150 gallon foam compound tank produced a staggering 32,000 litres/7,000 gallons of foam per minute.

Over time, international agreements between the various aviation regulating authorities were refined. Now every airport handling revenue-earning aircraft is required to provide an efficient fire and rescue service that is adequate to cope with the size and consequent fuel load of aircraft using its facilities. This means that a small provincial airfield served by the smallest commercial aircraft needs only a modest all-purpose 4x4 fire pump manned by a

four-man crew. At the other end of the scale, the largest and busiest international airports, such as Frankfurt, London Heathrow and JFK New York, are required to provide a range of permanently manned crash and rescue tenders that carry large quantities of firefighting foam and have fast all-terrain capability.

High-category airport fire engines, such as the Dutch Kronenberg tenders, are heavy three-axled vehicles, yet they perform impressively. Despite weighing in at approximately 30 tonnes, these vehicles can accelerate from 0 to 80kmh/50mph in just over 30 seconds. Each tender is capable of producing up to 9,000 litres/2,000 gallons of foam per minute through the roof-mounted guns or monitors.

Large airfield fire tenders have also been produced over the years for military use. The modern-day fire protection demands of some of the largest military aircraft, such as the Boeing B52, has led to the design of some very large fire engines, whose bulk is needed simply to

■ ABOVE *Two Simon airfield fire engines – a Protector foam and rescue tender (far left) and a Pacer rapid intervention vehicle (centre) – stand alongside an ambulance of the Nepal Civil Aviation Fire Service.*

■ BELOW LEFT *This executive jet crashed through the perimeter fence at Northolt Airfield, west London, and slewed into a van on an adjacent main road. Fortunately, there was no fire or serious injury as a result.*

■ BELOW RIGHT *A rescue helicopter stands by on the runway at Osaka, Japan.*

■ RIGHT *This airport 4x4 foam tender is a good example of a specialized aviation fire engine.*

■ BELOW RIGHT *A firefighter wearing a breathing set emerges from a smoke-filled aircraft during a training exercise.*

carry a sufficient quantity of foam and water. At its various bases around the world, the United States Air Force runs some monster fire engines, including the Oshkosh P-15 8x8 crash tender, whose twin 500hp diesel engines provide both drive and water-pumping power.

Time is unforgiving in any firefighting situation, but it is never more pressing than when an aircraft is on fire and large quantities of fuel are vulnerable and likely to intensify a fire. Airport fire stations are, therefore, usually located close to taxiways and runways so that the fire engines can get to a troubled aircraft as quickly as possible. Due to their sheer size, most large international airports have several fire stations located at strategic points. Foam tenders always form the first strike at any aircraft fire or accident, with the primary aim of rapidly knocking down or preventing a fire in order to allow other firefighters to get close into an aircraft to effect rescues.

On the training front, new levels of improved competency and skills are continually required of aviation firefighters to both match the increased fire risk of modern-day large aircraft and master the evolving operational capabilities of new airport fire engines. Alongside these developments have come improved training facilities, which recreate realistic live-fire training scenarios under safe and controlled conditions, and a better level of protection suits, breathing sets, hydraulic cutting and rescue gear, inflatable air bags and floodlighting.

With the prospect of a new generation of large twin-decked aircraft capable of carrying up to 600 passengers planned for the future, aviation firefighting and rescue arrangements will have to continue adapting as the twenty first century progresses.

TRANSPORTATION FIRES

An outbreak of fire involving any kind of transportation creates difficult and diverse operational problems for firefighters.

Most rail fires occur when a train is in service, usually through malfunction of equipment, perhaps in the restaurant galley, or from the careless disposal of a cigarette in a seat. The procedure for dealing with an on-train fire is pretty basic. The crew must stop the train and get everyone off as effectively as they can, and leave the firefighting to the experts whom they will have called out. If an emergency occurs in a remote spot, this can delay the fire brigades' response, as they will have to travel overland to reach the incident. This is where 4x4 fire engines are invaluable.

Trains are also at risk from fire following a derailment or collision involving diesel units or a tanker train containing flammable petro-chemical liquids.

Road vehicle fires can readily start when fuel or oil leaks or spills on to hot engine parts, such as an exhaust system or, in HGVs, buses and coaches, overheated brakes. They can also result from overheating then ignition of the wiring system due to an electrical fault. As elsewhere, the careless disposal of a cigarette is another cause of fire. Modern cars have a high content of plastic and foam seating materials, which burn fiercely once alight, as do some commercial loads. Following a crash, spilled fuel from the tank is likely to ignite in the presence of live electrical wires within the wreckage. Fire will almost certainly spread to other nearby vehicles.

Remote and inaccessible train and road crashes and fires are difficult enough to deal with, but when a fire occurs in a tunnel, the situation is even more hazardous. What makes tunnels so dangerous is that when heat and

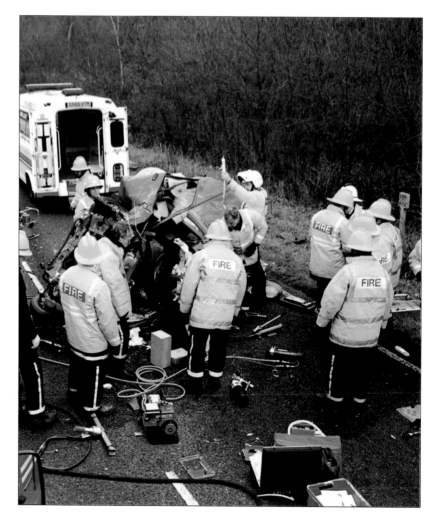

■ OPPOSITE ABOVE
AND BELOW *Fire crews
and medical teams work
together to free car
crash casualties.*

■ RIGHT *A London
firefighter surveys the
wreckage of the 1999
Ladbroke Grove
collision and fire which
involved two trains.
Many fatalities and
serious injuries were
caused with a number
of passengers requiring
extrication from
the wreckage.*

■ BELOW *Two specially
designed double-ended
Mercedes fire engines
pictured deep inside the
service tunnel of the
44 kilometre-/27 mile-
long Channel Tunnel.
Fire crews have ready
access to the running
railway lines linking
England and France.*

smoke fail to find any other escape route, they are vented relentlessly along the tunnel, posing dangers to travellers and firefighters alike. A flashover, which is dependent upon the rate of fire spread and the potential fire loading of whatever is burning, is always likely given that there will be a flow of air through a tunnel.

Modern road tunnels have escape staircases or refuges at frequent intervals, but older tunnels do not. While there are codes of safety practice, these older tunnels do not meet modern fire safety standards, and the costs to update them are very often considered to be prohibitive. Failing to take sufficient precautions can have tragic results. On 24 March 1999, a lorry caught fire as it travelled through the 11 kilometre/7 mile Mont Blanc Tunnel, beneath Europe's highest mountain. In the ensuing chaos 39 travellers were simply unable to escape. The fire burned for two days before firefighters overcame the intense conditions to eventually extinguish the inferno. The subsequent inquiry made 41 safety recommendations, including a complete redesign of the tunnel's smoke and ventilation system. Two years later, a serious fire broke out in a vehicle in the St Gotthard Tunnel in Switzerland, causing the death of 40 people.

Another catastrophic tunnel fire occurred on 18 November 1996 in the 44 kilometre/27 mile Channel Tunnel that links the United Kingdom with France. Only recently constructed, the

tunnel incorporated the latest fire safety features, yet fire still broke out, creating horrendous physical conditions for firefighters. On this occasion, the fire started in a lorry that had been loaded on to the train, the smoke being noticed only as the train entered the tunnel. The train came to a standstill some 13 kilometres/8 miles into the tunnel, by which time the priority was to get everyone off the train and into the safety tunnel that lies between the two rail tunnels; this safety tunnel is pressurized to prevent the ingress of smoke.

Before long, the fire had spread into other carriages of the train, igniting more vehicles and their contents. This resulted in a huge volume of thick smoke and a rapid rise in temperature, despite the automatic emergency smoke extraction system coming on.

Once the alarm had been raised, French and British fire crews responded from opposite ends of the service tunnel, driving double-ended fire engines specially designed for use in the Channel Tunnel. Although there were no serious casualties among the train passengers, the fire reached intense proportions and the firefighting effort became a hazardous and physically demanding operation that lasted for many hours. As the firefighting effort continued and more and more crews entered the tunnel,

they had to penetrate and endure a considerable heat barrier and high levels of toxic smoke. It was eight hours before the fire came under control.

At the height of the blaze, temperatures reached 1,000°C/1,830°F, which caused considerable collapse of some of the tunnel's structural sections. Such was the heat that some of the train's wagons became welded to the track. Kilometres of wiring and service ducting were destroyed, and it was many months before the Channel Tunnel was back in full operation, with improved fire and rescue procedures in place.

FIGHTING FIRES AT SEA

Fire on board ship can also turn into a nightmare scenario. The metal structure of the ship can quickly spread fire by conduction through bulkheads into unaffected areas. Ship fires usually start in the engine room, often with a broken fuel line spraying fuel on to hot machinery. All big ships now have a carbon dioxide or other inert gas flooding system, but this will only stifle a fire and prevent it spreading. Modern passenger ships also have sprinkler and automatic fire-detection systems installed, and the mega-cruise ships have fire-safety features on a par with those of new high-

■ ABOVE LEFT *The fire aboard the* Ebn Majid *in the English Channel in 1986 gave Dorset firefighters a hard time for several days and nights before they finally got the blaze under control.*

■ ABOVE RIGHT *The scale of this major rail accident is apparent from the widespread damage and wreckage involving two trains.*

rise buildings. Some of a ship's crew will have basic firefighting training, but ship fires require plenty of experienced firefighters, who can take some time to get on board.

Some of the perils of a ship fire are illustrated by events that took place on 28 January 1986, on board the *Ebn Majid* as it steamed up the English Channel. When traces of smoke were noticed coming from the hold of the ship, the carbon dioxide fire system was activated, but as the smoke continued to thicken, the ship's master requested urgent assistance. The *Ebn Majid* was towed into Weymouth Bay by the Royal Navy where a firefighting team from Dorset Fire Brigade boarded the vessel to find it was carrying a mixture of cattle feed, rubber and a variety of flammable chemicals. A huge firefighting operation was mounted, which lasted for four days and nights during which 120 breathing sets were in use, all needing to be continuously recharged. By the time the fire deep in the lower hold of the ship came under control, more than 8,000 hours had been logged by crews using 41 pumping engines and special vehicles on the nearby quayside, together with a number of fleet naval tugs surrounding the *Ebn Majid*. The cause of this fire is believed to have been spontaneous combustion.

With cruise ships, sheer numbers of passengers can create logistical problems. Also, fire may travel along the narrow below-deck corridors to create conditions from which it can be difficult to escape. Typical was the fate of the Italian cruise liner *Achille Lauro*, off the North African coast. When a fire broke out in the engine room on 30 December 1994, the 1,000 passengers and crew had to abandon ship and take to lifeboats and rafts. Three passengers lost their lives during the dramatic rescue operation, and the *Achille Lauro* was left a blackened and smouldering ruin.

■ BELOW LEFT *The aftermath of a helicopter crash showing a foam carpet surrounding the aircraft and fire engines still in attendance.*

■ BELOW RIGHT *Against a background of thick smoke this modern fireboat blasts two powerful water jets on to a burning vessel.*

FIRE STATIONS AND FIREHOUSES

Although many fire stations, or firehouses as they are known in the United States, are relatively modern structures, some have been in continuous service for a long time, adapting to changes in firefighting practice over the years. The 132-year-old Clerkenwell station, for example, is still a front line station of the London Fire Brigade. Here, as in a number of other older fire stations in Britain, the original Victorian layout is clearly visible, and a number of fittings are still in place on the walls and ceiling where formerly harnesses and other linkages used for the horse-drawn fire engines of earlier times were hung. In those far-off days, firemen worked incredible 24-hour shifts, living on the job with their families in two-room flats above the station itself. Whole families of firemen's children were brought up using the fire station drill yard as their

■ ABOVE *Crews of the Metropolitan (London) Fire Brigade on their horse-drawn fire engines line up on Southwark fire station's forecourt, in about 1895.*

■ FAR LEFT *A traditional American timber fire station (firehouse) incorporates a lookout and bell tower. This late nineteenth-century example is in Ridgeway, Colorado, USA.*

■ LEFT *This early nineteenth-century timber firehouse, in Nevada City, California, USA, has a lookout in the roof, with a bell on top.*

■ ABOVE *Seven London Fire Brigade motor fire engines and their brass-helmeted crews make a brave sight in front of the Southwark Headquarters c. 1923.*

playground, and the station commander had the regular duty of inspecting the family accommodation to ensure it was being kept in clean order.

Some old fire stations are housed within grand surroundings. When King George VI opened the London Fire Brigade's new five-storey headquarters at Lambeth in July 1937, the ground floor had seven bays along a 64m/210ft frontage. The entrance hall contained a bronze-and-marble memorial dedicated to all the brigade officers and men who had lost their lives in action. Ironically, the site headquarters was formerly a riverside wharf where a serious fire in 1918 killed seven brigade members.

Today, city-centre and urban fire stations tend to house a number of fire engines, which stand in bays ready for action. The central office, or watchroom, is situated close to the fire engine bays. It is called the watchroom because in pre-telephone days members of the public would run to the station's permanently manned office in order to raise the alarm. Nowadays, the watchroom houses a modern communication system with various links to the control and despatch centre, often situated many miles away, and generally serves as the nerve centre for the station. The station is mobilized to fire and emergency calls either by hard copy off the printer or by a broadcast radio message.

■ BELOW LEFT *Three modern American fire engines show off their colourful liveries.*

■ BELOW RIGHT *This three-bay firehouse in Alexandria, Virginia, USA, dates from the late nineteenth century.*

Fire stations in large towns and cities are almost exclusively manned by full-time fire-fighters and so need to have sleeping and living accommodation for on-duty crews. Other facilities include lockers, showers, laundry, lecture room, equipment storage, breathing-set servicing, including an air compressor for recharging cylinders, a gymnasium or fitness training area and a muster bay.

Outside there is a fuelling point and covered wash-down area for cleaning the fire engines. Much of the routine inspection and maintenance work on the hundreds of items of equipment carried on the vehicles are conducted out here. Many larger urban stations also incorporate a training-drill tower structure that consists of several floors with windows at various levels for training sessions. Other training facilities are likely to include a building containing confined-space crawling galleries, with various obstacles, into which heat and cosmetic smoke can be introduced for breathing-set training. In some stations, firefighters with paramedic skills crew an

■ ABOVE *In Great Whale Town, Quebec, Canada, an unassuming two-bay fire station is part of a small hotel complex.*

■ LEFT *An aerial ladder is being checked over in the fire-engine repair workshop of Boston Fire Department, USA.*

■ RIGHT *Opened in 1992, the impressive British Airports Authority Fire Service's headquarters and central fire station is situated close to the runways and taxiways at London Heathrow Airport.*

emergency ambulance, which is stationed alongside the fire engines.

Fire stations in rural areas are generally much smaller than their urban counterparts, needing only to house one or two fire engines. Their structure tends to be simple, often single storey, and with very basic facilities. In addition to a watchroom, many rural fire stations have an external drill tower and yard area for ladder, hose and pump-training sessions, together with a building in which basic heat and breathing-set training can be carried out. Rural stations are normally manned by part-time retained crews or even volunteers who only attend the station for a call-out or a training session.

A feature of all modern fire stations is an area of the drill yard dedicated to road accident extrication practice. Here there will be several cars, usually in various stages of demolition following regular training sessions in the speedy use of powerful cutting and spreading equipment.

In addition to their primary function as integral parts of the fire emergency service, fire stations are increasingly used as a focus in the community for various fire safety education efforts. Displays of good fire safety practice set against examples of some of the preventable causes of fire are used to good effect by firefighters during visits by schools and various other local groups.

■ BELOW *Kent Fire Brigade's new eight-bay fire station at Ashford, England, is close to the British terminal of the Channel Tunnel.*

FIREFIGHTING UNIFORMS

In the eighteenth and nineteenth centuries firemen's liveried uniforms were colourful but totally impractical, conceived more as ready identification of a particular insurance brigade than as effective protection against the physical dangers of firefighting. Even when more powerful pumps and water jets meant that firemen could work more closely to a fire and sometimes even inside burning buildings, they remained poorly protected against the dangers of scorching heat and falling masonry and timber as a burning building progressively weakened and fell apart.

Some of the first practical and radical improvements in firemen's uniforms came in 1824 when James Braidwood, the newly appointed Master of Fire Engines in Edinburgh, replaced the colourful frock coats of the recently amalgamated insurance companies with double-breasted wool tunics. He added leather helmets and knee-length boots to the new uniform. When Braidwood moved to London, in 1832, to take charge of the capital's fire brigade he continued making improvements to the style and effectiveness of his firefighters' uniforms and introduced silk neckerchiefs to prevent sparks from falling down their necks.

By the mid-nineteenth century, brass military-style helmets had become popular firefighting headgear in many parts of Europe. American firemen continued to use leather helmets along with longer-style bunker coats, which, with various improvements in fabric and design, have remained the preferred American pattern to the present day. In Europe and elsewhere, brass helmets were replaced in the 1930s by cork and plastic versions following several incidents where firefighters were killed after their helmet made contact with a live wire

dangling from a fire-damaged ceiling. During World War II, firefighters on both sides of the conflict exchanged their peacetime helmets for steel military-style versions, but the rest of the standard firemen's wartime uniform was little changed from that of pre-war years.

■ LEFT *The early uniform worn by Paris firemen (Sapeurs-Pompiers), c.1860, indicates the force's military origins. Around this time, brass helmets became a commonplace part of firefighting uniforms.*

■ BELOW *Due to the increasing risk of electrocution, in 1934 brass helmets were replaced with a compressed-cork version, seen here on the left.*

■ OPPOSITE BOTTOM *London firefighters display various uniforms worn from 1866 (right) through to the current uniform (left).*

Significant changes and improvements to firefighting uniforms began to be made during the 1980s following the introduction of technology that produced the first flame-retardant fabrics and fibres specially designed for firefighting use. This has led to great advances in the design style of firefighting uniforms, which now embraces head-to-toe clothing protection and is termed personal protective equipment (PPE).

■ ABOVE LEFT *This c.1936 London Fire Brigade uniform remained in operational use until the 1970s.*

■ ABOVE MIDDLE *A Japanese firefighter in military-style uniform.*

■ ABOVE RIGHT *Modern firefighting suits provide maximum protection.*

One particularly serious British fire in November 1987 provided a springboard for uniform improvement. A sudden flashover up an escalator engulfed evening commuters at London's Kings Cross Underground station and 31 people died, including a fire officer. The subsequent inquiry made a number of recommendations, including the improvement of the level of personal protection for firemen facing such awful circumstances.

PROTECTIVE CLOTHING

Today's firefighting tunics and trousers incorporate a durable outer shell for physical protection, a moisture barrier that prevents hot water and hazardous liquid penetration, together with an in-built thermal barrier. With helmets and boots they achieve a blend of maximum protection against high temperatures and other dangers, while providing a maximum level of comfort when worn for lengthy periods in a hot and unpleasant environment.

Helmets have also been improved and are now constructed from toughened plastics, with

■ ABOVE LEFT *Japanese firefighters in breathing sets and lightweight protective suits await orders.*

■ ABOVE RIGHT *A Japanese firefighting team in full protective clothing and breathing masks hold a high-powered hose nozzle.*

■ BELOW *Japanese firefighters in full uniform parade.*

the provision of a swing-down visor. Recently developed space-age materials have helped to reduce the overall weight of helmets while increasing facial and neck protection, and improving overall wearer comfort levels. Some helmet models have a wrap-around shape with a pull-down visor built into the structure. Fire-retardant material is also used in the manufacture of gloves and anti-flash hoods, which are particularly important when working with the risk of flashover and the resulting sudden high temperatures.

Modern boot design incorporates maximum foot-protection features, including reinforced toecaps, special soles and a sealing process that prevents the ingress of any liquids. The last feature is especially important in situations where these liquids could contain run-off from a hazardous chemical incident.

The conventional firefighting suit is not at all practical for protracted firefighting operations in bush and forest areas, which occur in summer months and can go on for weeks at a time. This work is physically demanding enough, without the extra burden of high ambient weather temperatures. The wild land firefighting coverall suit was designed to overcome all these problems. It

■ RIGHT *Senior officers and firemen of the Vienna Fire Brigade in firefighting uniforms of 1920.*

reduces heat stress by providing a tough, yet comfortable, highly breathable suit that offers short-term protection against heat and flames.

Modern uniforms are increasingly subject to a range of stringent international testing standards across the various types of operational use, including those for general firefighting, wild land fires, hazardous materials and non-fire rescue. Modern fire suits are designed to be regularly laundered under strictly controlled procedures. In Europe, these standards have been set out in a recent EU directive. American standards have gone a little further and ensure that any build-up of dangerous hydrocarbons and other harmful toxins are removed during the PPE cleaning process.

Firefighting uniforms are one area where modern technology has been used to lighten

■ BELOW LEFT *Modern uniforms protect firemen from the fierce heat of flames.*

■ BELOW RIGHT *Heavily protected Japanese firefighters prepare to mount a foam attack during a training exercise.*

the physical load upon firefighters, while providing the maximum level of personal protection as crews work in a hazardous and challenging environment. It is no surprise, however, to find that old-style fire helmets, including those made of polished brass, are still retained by many brigades for use during special ceremonial occasions.

FIREFIGHTER TRAINING

Firefighters undergo rigorous training to prepare them for the physical demands of the job and to use a range of tools and aids, as well as some high-tech equipment. They must be able to work quickly, efficiently and calmly in stressful conditions, as a part of a team or individually. They also have to work in all weather conditions, often in a dangerous environment. Working at height off ladders or in confined spaces in complete darkness must hold no fears, and a strong mental constitution is necessary as all firefighters witness tragedy and suffering during their front-line work.

TRAINING PROCEDURES

Usually brigades are staffed by full-time professional firemen and part-time retained firemen. Professional recruits attend an intensive basic course that includes theoretical work, study and plenty of practical drill. The latter involves learning how to handle virtually every item of firefighting and rescue equipment – fire pumps, hose, ladders, extinguishers, lighting, knots and lines, resuscitators, cutting

■ ABOVE *Firefighters practise their skills during a pump and ladder drill exercise.*

■ FAR LEFT *Fire crews work with two turntable ladders on a training tower in Zian Province, China.*

■ LEFT *Under the watchful eye of their instructor, recruit firefighters practise the carry-down of a rescued 'casualty' on an extension ladder.*

■ OPPOSITE *The New York Fire Training Centre, USA, has extensive fire-training buildings at its disposal.*

■ ABOVE LEFT *Paris firemen scale the outside face of a training drill tower, c.1920.*

■ ABOVE MIDDLE *A German fireman prepares to leap from the first floor in this jumping sheet drill, c.1910.*

■ ABOVE RIGHT *German firefighters' training sessions included a rescue chute drill, c.1910.*

and lifting gear and a range of other items. Recruits also have to qualify in advanced first aid and casualty-handling techniques.

Once recruits have satisfactorily completed the basic training they are ready to become part of an operational firefighting and rescue unit for a probationary period. They will ride a fire engine as crew members and gain experience from the wide range of incidents they attend. Ongoing training continues throughout a firefighter's career, and in order to maintain strength and stamina most have access to fitness-training equipment, which is often provided at their fire stations.

Breathing-set training is critical for all firemen, as there are few structural fire situations where sets are not worn. Personal breathing sets enable firefighters to survive and work in thick, choking smoke. Regular training in the use of this crucial piece of equipment is carried out inside a special building that is often attached to the fire station. Incorporating several floors, the building can be fitted with a number of different and varying obstacles and hazards. It can also be heated to create a humid atmosphere and filled with cosmetic smoke. Crews undergoing training are given objectives such as the location of a 'body' or

other simulated casualty, during which they must exercise all the safety and control features of breathing-set operation.

SPECIALIST TRAINING

Firefighters must also learn how to deal with the nightmarish eventuality of a 'flashover', a situation where unburned gases suddenly ignite in a ball of fire. Two distinct forms of training have been developed for this. The first type burns carbonaceous materials (usually chipboard) in steel containers to create realistic fire, heat and smoke conditions that allow crews to both understand and experience real fire behaviour patterns. Unfortunately, these carbonaceous units take some time to set up and can only be used for one training burn at a time.

Gas-fired training simulator buildings have been introduced in recent years to provide readily repeatable 'hot-fire' training. These brick or steel structures incorporate a number of domestic scenarios designed to represent fires in a cooking pan, a settee, a television set and a bed, as well as a flashover facility. All the fires are controlled via a computer program linked to gas and temperature monitoring, and full ventilation in the event of an emergency shutdown. Such realistic but safe hot-fire

training enables firefighters to learn how to recognize the early onset of a flashover and to perfect various water-cooling techniques to reduce their likelihood.

Another type of regular training is designed to hone extrication skills using heavy-duty cutting gear. Firefighters are often called to attend serious traffic and other types of accident to free trapped people speedily. Cars are often compacted in a crash, so releasing people involves cutting off car roofs, removing steering columns and taking apart sections of bodywork, often alongside a paramedic. The training involves working together as a team as quickly as possible and without causing the casualty any further distress.

Once qualified, a firefighter's career path can lead towards promotion via examinations in conjunction with suitable experience, making it possible for young professional recruits to aspire to the very highest ranks in the service. They can acquire further specialist skills such as driving, aerial ladder operation, fire safety, forensic fire investigation and line-rescue qualifications. Fire service drivers are trained to handle heavy vehicles while travelling at considerable speeds to an emergency. They need a high level of awareness and anticipation in all traffic and weather conditions on a

■ ABOVE LEFT *Line rescue training for urban firefighters includes rock climbing and abseiling sessions carried out on moorland cliffs and rock faces.*

■ ABOVE RIGHT *Shielded by the cooling protection of a water spray hose line, two recruit firefighters get close in to flames during a live fire training exercise in a gas-fired simulator.*

■ LEFT *Japanese firefighters undergo line rescue training involving traverses and descents from a variety of heights and positions.*

■ RIGHT *A USAF firefighter demonstrates the water flow through a hose line.*

variety of highways ranging from main network trunk routes through to the most narrow and twisting country lanes.

In rural and low-population areas, fire cover is provided mostly by part-time retained firefighters from the local community. These firemen live and work close to the fire station they serve. Recruits attend basic training, often spread over evenings and weekends. Working with hose lines, pumps and ladders they learn how to use the same equipment as that carried on professionally manned fire engines. On completion of their basic training, a recruit retainee officially joins the strength of the local fire station but continues to follow their normal occupation and lifestyle. When needed for a turnout, at any time of the day of night, they are called to the fire station by pager.

Firefighters attached to rural and country fire stations usually come together once a week for a continuation training session, which might involve a drill session using the pumps, ladders, breathing sets and other equipment carried on the fire engine. There is also the important task of equipment checks and routine maintenance. Every item of firefighting and rescue equipment must be in working order when it is taken from the fire engine locker at an incident – as someone's life may well depend upon it.

■ BELOW *New York recruit firefighters still have scaling/hook ladder training. Originally used to gain access into buildings from narrow alleyways, these ladders are rarely used operationally now, but the training helps to instil confidence in preparation for working at height.*

Fire brigades have a long and proud history of reliable service to the community at large, which, coupled with a high level of excitement, drama, action, and some excellent career prospects, contributes to making the work of a firefighter a very special calling. Full-time professionals and part-time firefighters throughout the world undoubtedly derive much job satisfaction from their work, a fact that is borne out by very low personnel wastage, with few firefighters leaving the service before their normal retirement date.

COMMUNICATIONS AND CALL-OUTS

Fire service control and communications centres are a vital, yet unseen, part of firefighting and rescue operations, for they handle every emergency call-out and the mobilization of each fire engine, and have the overall control of each incident, large or small. Taking advantage of the latest developments in new technology, they ensure a rapid response to any type of situation – a far cry from the early days of horse-drawn manual pumps when a fire engine's turnout speed was likely to be dictated by the availability of the nearest borrowed horse.

When fire brigades were first established in the eighteenth century, the only way to call out a fire engine was for a member of the public to run or ride to the fire station and alert the crew. Many brigades installed a large brass bell outside the station for raising the alarm. During the nineteenth century, a bugle call proved a popular method of calling nearby volunteer firefighters to the fire station to man the pump. The arrival of street fire alarms and the electric telegraph greatly speeded up call-out times.

In the mid-twentieth century the widespread use of radio for fire service operations was in

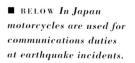
■ ABOVE *London Fire Brigade switchboard and watchroom, c.1909, received all fire calls and despatched fire engines.*

■ BELOW *In Japan motorcycles are used for communications duties at earthquake incidents.*

its infancy. The state of fire service communications technology at that time can be illustrated by a brief historical reflection from the intense 1940–1 London Blitz of World War II. During this period of continual enemy air raids, all the mobilizing activity to send pumping fire engines to the thousands of separate fire incidents each day and night was done manually by the control centre's fire service operators, using written messages and tallies on boards to represent fire engines. Most of the urgent operational messages between the local commanders at major fires and the central control rooms were carried by teams of motorcycle despatch riders, who managed to keep going even while the bombs were falling.

In modern fire departments around the world the development of computers and communications technology in the late twentieth century led progressively to the centralization of emergency-call handling in control centres that were far removed from the noise and drama of front-line firefighting operations. When an emergency incident occurs, the fire brigade is

COMMUNICATIONS AND CALL-OUTS

■ LEFT *Before sounding this street alarm, a woman uses her shoe to break the protective glass covering c.1920. The alarm triggered a panel in the nearest fire station giving the location of the alarm point.*

alerted after a member of the public calls the national emergency number using the public telephone network or a mobile phone. The call is quickly routed via the public telephone network to a fire brigade operator at the fire control centre for that particular area. The operator is trained to calm the caller, if necessary, and obtain a clear address or location for the incident, together with the caller's phone number. Meanwhile, the network operator monitors the conversation to check that a complete address is given. In the case of a distressed caller hanging up before giving complete details, the operator can trace the call and pinpoint the caller's address or location.

The control operator keys all the call information into the computer system as the caller is speaking. The system immediately identifies the nearest available fire engine to respond to the call and the precise fire-risk category of the address. When the location is a factory or large warehouse, the response will involve several fire engines, usually including an aerial ladder. A single pump would be

■ BELOW *An operator takes an emergency call, on an old-fashioned switchboard, at a centralized fire control centre.*

despatched to a rural property. Within seconds, the call-out order is sent to the relevant fire station's printer giving the precise location of the incident and the type of premises believed to be involved. Some mobilizing systems also provide vital information such as basic details of a building's layout, the location of the nearest street hydrants and the presence of special risks, such as chemicals or hazardous materials. In some brigades, the address information is broadcast throughout the fire station as the crew turn out.

In a permanently manned station the crew can be on the way to the fire or emergency within a minute of a call being received at the control centre many miles away. When a call is to a rural or country fire station, central control activates the personal pagers, or alerters, of the retained firefighters, who live and work near the station. They will immediately dash to the fire station and be on their way within several minutes. As the crew turn out, the crew commander acknowledges acceptance of the call, by either sending a radio message or using

on-board push-button technology. Staff at the control centre continue to monitor an incident through to its conclusion. All radio traffic comes to control via a direct radio link with the mobile control centre at the scene of an incident. If upon arrival at a scene the first crew are confronted with a major fire or accident situation, they immediately request assistance and further fire engines will be despatched to the scene. At this point the control centre operators assess the reduced overall fire cover for the area and, if necessary, order distant unaffected crews to temporarily cover depleted fire stations. If the original incident continues to develop, control will mobilize any further urgent requests for equipment, such as extra breathing sets, floodlighting, foam, heavy lifting gear, refreshments and, once the incident is under control, relief crews. Control centre operators also liaise with their opposite numbers in the police and paramedic control centres, so that each service is aware of the various incidents occurring, and which might at any time need a tri-service response.

■ BELOW *All brigades in industrialized countries, including smaller regional ones, have computerized call-handling and mobilizing centres to guarantee a fast and efficient response to all emergencies.*

REVOLUTIONARY DEVELOPMENTS

Recent radio developments have revolutionized fire service operations. All crew members are equipped with a personal radio so they can stay in touch with each other at the scene. At a major incident, the multiple channels of these radios allow the mobile control unit to speak to the commanders of the various sectors of the fire and to other firefighters at work across the site. Radio links are also essential for relaying critical information at speed. When an emergency involves an identified hazardous chemical, for example, control immediately accesses a special database to obtain priority information on the substance. This data is then relayed via a radio link to the printer on board the mobile control centre at the scene, enabling the officer in charge to ensure the firefighters adopt correct and safe procedures for dealing with the chemical concerned.

Many large and busy fire brigades use a series of coded radio messages to cover a range of particular operational requests and situations. This shortens the transmission time and reduces the overall radio traffic, which can be critical when a number of fire engines are deployed at fires and emergencies at different locations at the same time.

■ BELOW *The nerve centre of every fire brigade is its control room. Here, staff of the West Midlands' (England) command and control suite handle all the brigade's fire and emergency activities.*

GLOSSARY

Apparatus Generic American term for a fire engine.

Aerial Ladder A telescopic steel ladder made up of sections, which rotates around a turntable mounted either at the rear or middle of a fire engine chassis. It has either a crew bucket or cage at top able to provide rescue and project a water jet into buildings at upper levels. In USA, some aerial ladders are tractor-drawn articulated units with a steered rear axle.

Aerial Ladder Platform (ALP) Fire engine with cage for high-rise firefighting and rescue with several folding telescopic booms which rotate through 360 degrees. Has an auxiliary ladder alongside booms.

Airfield Crash Tender Powerful high-capacity foam tender with all-wheel drive designed for aviation and airport firefighting and rescue.

Air masks and bottles US term for compressed air or oxygen breathing sets, and air/oxygen cylinders.

Brake Horsepower (bhp) The power developed by an engine as measured by a dynamometer.

Branch The nozzle end of a firefighting hose line.

Breathing Apparatus European term for breathing sets.

Chemical Incident/Hazmat Unit Fire engine which carries protective suits and equipment for dealing with nuclear/ biological/chemical spills, leakages and subsequent decontamination.

Control/Despatch Centre Geographically centralized, computer-controlled communications base that handles all emergency calls, mobilizes fire engines and has overall control of major incidents.

Control Unit Fire engine designed to operate as mobile command centre at fires and other emergency incidents.

Emergency Tender Fire engine which carries a wide range of cutting, lifting, and heavy rescue equipment, virtually a travelling workshop with self-contained power supplies for tools and lighting.

Engine US term for a fire engine with the primary purpose of pumping water and providing hose lines. Also known as a pumper.

Fire Engine Generic term for all types of firefighting and rescue vehicles.

Fire Station/Firehouse Building which houses fire engines, has accommodation for firefighters and some training facilities.

Foam Tender Fire engine which produces and projects large quantities of foam on to liquid fires involving fuels and petrochemicals.

Forward Control/Cab Over Engine A cab directly over the engine unit.

Hazmat Denote hazardous materials including those of a toxic, corrosive or irritant nature.

Hose Usually in 22.8m/75ft lengths and with either snap-together or screw couplings. Is stowed coiled or flaked on fire engines.

Hose Layer Fire engine capable of laying out up to a mile of pre-flaked hose at speed during major firefighting operations, from a major water source to the scene of the fire.

Hose Line Lengths of hose joined together taking water from a fire engine to the scene of the fire.

Hose Reels Small, 2.5cm/1in diameter, rubber hose, coiled on circular drums on each side or at the rear of most pumps/ water tenders. Fed from an onboard water tank and used to provide an immediate attack on a small fire.

Hydraulic Platform First-generation, high-rise fire engine consisting of several folding, hydraulically operated booms with a cage at the top.

Pump European term for a fire engine which carries crew of six, pumps water, carries breathing sets, ladders and firefighting and rescue gear. Also the term for the separate inbuilt machinery that pressurizes and propels water from the fire engine through hoses to the fire.

Pumper US equivalent of pump.

Pump Escape European term for Pump which also carries a 15m/50ft wooden, wheeled escape ladder with the primary purpose of performing a rescue.

Rescue Truck US term for Emergency Tender.

Special Service Call Any non-fire emergency such as a road or rail crash, accident, chemical spill or leak, animal rescue, or humanitarian duty.

Steamer Fire engine with coal-fired boiler producing steam to drive the water pump to produce a water jet.

Thermal Imaging Camera Hand-held electronic device which allows fire crews to see clearly through smoke.

Tiller Long-wheelbase, USA aerial-ladder fire engine with a rear-axle steering position to assist the vehicle to negotiate tight corners.

Truck US term for apparatus (fire engine) which carries ladders, forcible entry and other heavy gear.

Tower Ladder A US aerial ladder with a fitted cage at its head with fixed hose.

Turntable Ladder European equivalent of US aerial/tower ladder able to rotate 360 degrees around a turntable base.

Water Carrier/Tanker Fire engine with large-capacity water tank used to ferry firefighting water in rural areas.

Water Fog Finely atomized water mist produced at hose branch to protect firefighters from the intense, radiated heat of a fire.

Water Tender A rural, pumping fire engine with 13.5m/45ft ladder.

PICTURE CREDITS

The publishers would like to thank the following for their kind permission to reproduce their photographs:

AKG 14 top. **Alamy** 36–37, 65 top right, 84 top, 87 top and 117 top. **Andrew Henry** 56 bottom.
Bob Dubbert 50 centre. **Bridgeman Art Library** 14 bottom left and bottom right, 15 top right and bottom,
18 bottom left and bottom right, 19 bottom, 20 top left, 21 bottom, 22 bottom, 23 bottom right, 24 top left, 26 top,
42 bottom and 114 top. **Code Red** 10, 11, 31 top left, 33 bottom left, 62 bottom, 80 bottom and 97 bottom.
Corbis 19 top left, 93 top. **Dave Stewardson** 34 top right **Firepix International** 30 top, 62 top left and top centre,
63 top right, 78 top right, 79 bottom right and bottom left, 81 top, 82 top, 886, 90 top, 94 bottom left, 97 top,
100 bottom, 102 top, 104 bottom right, 105 bottom, 112 bottom, 115 top centre, 116 (all), 117 bottom right,
118 bottom left, 119 bottom, 121 top left, 122 bottom and 123 bottom. **Gary Chapman** 96 top and bottom.
Iveco 35 bottom and 67 centre bottom. **Jerry Sires** 51 bottom, 55 bottom, 56 top, 57 top, 65 top left and bottom,
67 bottom, 95 bottom, 103 top and 111 bottom left **Keith Wardell** 53 top right and 57 bottom.
National Motor Museum 45 top right, 46 top, 48 bottom, 49 bottom, 52 bottom, 60 bottom left.
Neil Wallington 12–13, 16 (all), 17 top, 18 top, 19 top right, 21 top right, 23 top right, centre and bottom left,
24 top right and bottom, 253 top and bottom, 27 top and bottom, 28 top, 29 top, 31 bottom, 32 bottom left and bottom right,
33 top, 34 top left and bottom right, 35 top left and top right, 38 bottom right, 41 bottom left and bottom right,
43 top left and bottom, 46 bottom, 47 bottom, 48 top, 49 centre, 50 top and bottom, 53 bottom, 57 centre, 59 centre right,
61 top left and bottom left, 62 top right, 63 bottom, 64 bottom, 66 top and bottom, 71 top left, second left from top,
bottom left and bottom right, 72–73, 74 top, 75 top, 76 top and bottom, 77 (all), 78 top left and bottom, 79 top,
80 top, 81 bottom left and bottom right, 82 bottom, 83 top and bottom, 84 bottom, 85 top and bottom, 86 left and right,
87 bottom, 89 top and bottom, 90 bottom, 91, 92, 94 top and bottom right, 95 top, 99 top and bottom, 100 top, 101,
104 top and bottom left, 106 top and bottom, 107 top and bottom, 108 top left and top right, 109 bottom left, 110 top,
111 top, 113 top and bottom, 114 bottom, 115 top left, top right and bottom, 117 bottom left, 118 top and bottom right,
120 top right, 121 bottom, 122 top, 123 top, 124 top and bottom, and 125. **Shane Mackichan** 54 top and bottom,
55 top and 105 top. **Shaun Ryan** 67 top right. **Spectrum** 53 top left. **Travel Ink** 17 bottom, 110 bottom left and right,
111 bottom right, 112 top and 120 top left. **TRH** 20 top right and bottom, 21 top left, 22 top, 26 bottom, 28 bottom,
29 bottom, 30 bottom, 31 top right, 32 top, 33 bottom right, 34 centre left, 38 top and bottom left, 39 top and bottom,
40 top and bottom, 41 top, 42 top, 43 top right, 44 top and bottom, 45 top left and bottom, 47 top, 49 top, 51 top,
52 top left and top right, 58 top and bottom, 59 top, bottom left and bottom right, 60 top and centre,
61 top right and bottom right, 63 top left, 64 top, 67 top left, 68, 69 top and bottom, 70 (all),
71 top right and third from top left, 74 bottom, 75 bottom, 93 bottom, 98, 102 bottom, 103 centre and bottom,
109 bottom right, 119 top left, top centre and top right, 121 top right.

I NDEX